WHAT

A WAY

GO

What a Way to Go

Fabulous Funerals of the Famous and Infamous

ADELE Q. BROWN

CHRONICLE BOOKS

ACKNOWLEDGMENTS

I am extraordinarily grateful to my editors at High Tide Press, Peter C. Jones, Lisa MacDonald, and Roger Straus, for their guidance and encouragement; and to Steve Mockus of Chronicle Books for his faith in this project. Maggie Berkvist deserves kudos for her splendid photo research. I am blessed with family and friends who eagerly supplied me with research materials, ideas, and favorite memorials, and I thank all of them for their cheery efforts on what otherwise might have been a gloomy topic. Particular thanks go to Anne E. Brown, Christopher L. Brown, David S. Brown Jr., Robert L. Brown, Carl Burton, Patricia Davis, Amy and Dennis Metnick, Ada Nelken, Nina Nelken, Christina Rockrise, and especially my nurturing neighbors Bob and Myrna Greenhall. I am most indebted to my husband, Dan Nelken, whose understanding was cosmic when I transformed my office into a tomb, and myself into an apparition, while working on this book. His support and love keep me happily grounded in this world.

—A. Q. B.

LIBRARY OF CONGRESS CATALOGING-IN-PUBLICATION DATA AVAILABLE.

ISBN 0-8118-2750-X

PRINTED IN CHINA.

DESIGNED BY SARA SCHNEIDER

DISTRIBUTED IN CANADA BY RAINCOAST BOOKS
9050 SHAUGHNESSY STREET
VANCOUVER, BRITISH COLUMBIA V6P 6E5

10 9 8 7 6 5 4 3 2 1

CHRONICLE BOOKS LLC
85 SECOND STREET
SAN FRANCISCO, CALIFORNIA 94105

WWW.CHRONICLEBOOKS.COM

CREDITS:

AP/PETER DEJONG: PAGE 145. AP/WIDE WORLD PHOTOS: PAGES 29, 54, 55, 77. ARNOLD NEWMAN/LIASON: PAGE 156. BAD BOY RECORDS: PAGE 97. BALDWIN H. WARD/CORBIS/BETTMANN: PAGE 131. CAPITOL RECORDS: PAGE 107. CLARIN CONTENIDOS: PAGES 99, 103. CORBIS/BETTMANN: PAGES 15, 16, 19, 43, 50, 61, 83, 102, 118, 130, 132, 139, 161, 162. CORBIS/REUTERS: PAGE 30. COVER/LUIS MORENO: PAGE 33. CULVER PICTURES: PAGES 35, 167. DENNIS STOCK/MAGNUM PHOTOS: PAGE 89. FDR LIBRARY: PAGE 124. HULTON/ARCHIVE/EXPRESS NEWSPAPERS: PAGES 28, 112, 117, 123. HULTON/ARCHIVE/LAMBERT STUDIO: PAGE 86. HULTON/ARCHIVE/POPPERFOTO: PAGES 11, 49, 71. HULTON/ARCHIVE/ REUTERS/FAITH SARIBAS: PAGE 72. HULTON/ARCHIVE/REUTERS/ JEROME DELAY: PAGE 144. HULTON/ARCHIVE: PAGES 23, 56, 65, 93, 111, 149, 155, 169, 175. NATIONAL PARK SERVICE/EDISON NATIONAL HISTORIC SITE: PAGES 38, 39. NEW YORK DAILY NEWS: PAGES 94, 138. PARAMOUNT PICTURES: PAGE 59. TAYLOR/CORBIS: PAGE 140.

HEADLINES USED FOR "NEWS OF THE DAY" FROM THE *NEW YORK TIMES*

For My Parents
~ In Memoriam ~

EVELYN LOVETT BROWN   DAVID SPRINGER BROWN

(MARCH 6, 1920–MAY 22, 1967)   (DECEMBER 27, 1915–MARCH 11. 1996)

CONTENTS

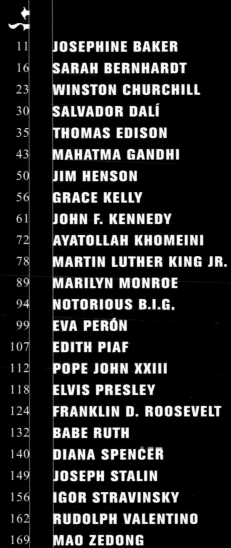

JOSEPHINE BAKER

"La Baker"

June 3, 1906–April 12, 1975

"France made me what I am. They gave me their hearts. Surely I can give them my life."

∿ **BAKER,** IN BANANAS, CIRCA 1920s

VITAL STATISTICS

AGE AT DEATH: 68

CAUSE OF DEATH: Cerebral hemorrhage

SURVIVORS: Her estranged husband, bandleader Jo Bouillon; twelve adopted children; and her sister, Margaret Wallace

CLOSE CALLS: In 1941 Baker nearly died following an emergency hysterectomy, after giving birth to a stillborn child in a Moroccan hospital, and news of her death was prematurely broadcast on Allied radio.

HER LIFE

Josephine Baker was born in St. Louis, Missouri, as Freda Josephine MacDonald, an illegitimate child of an African American mother. The light-skinned girl, ostracized by her family, was sent at age seven to work as a maid, laboring for a series of physically and sexually abusive employers. She was married by age thirteen and divorced a year later.

Her love of theater bloomed after she was exposed to vaudeville by one of her early employers, a family of musicians. She frequented the Booker Theater in St. Louis, endearing herself to blues singer Clara Smith, who quickly became her mentor and lover. During her teens, Baker traveled through the South with Smith's touring company, eventually ending up in Philadelphia, where she met her second husband, Billy Baker. She later left him to audition for Eubie Blake and Noble Sissle's *Shuffle Along,* a hugely successful all-black revue that was looking for talent for its touring company. Baker was cast at her second audition.

Blake and Sissle wrote a part in the 1924 new revue, *Chocolate Dandies,* specifically for Baker. Although that musical was short-lived, Baker's stage presence drew the attention of nightclub promoters and she was cast in the chorus of the famous Harlem nightclub The Plantation. It was here that Baker discovered her great comedic talent, mugging for the audience while dancing provocatively.

Her big break came when impresario Caroline Dudley Reagan cast the eighteen-year-old Baker in her all-black show, *La Revue Nègre,* which opened in Paris in 1925 at the Théâtre de Champs-Élysées. Earning $200 a week and wearing only feathers, Baker performed in two sensational numbers accompanied by jazz clarinetist Sidney Bechet. She toured with the production as far as Berlin, where she was courted with offers by movie directors and nightclub promoters. She chose the most lucrative of these options, leaving *La Revue Nègre* for a starring role in the Folies-Bergère in Paris.

At just twenty years old, Josephine Baker became the toast of the City of Light, celebrated by and hobnobbing with the highest of high society in 1920s Europe. Baker exuded a style all her own and capitalized on it through wily self-promotion—endorsing products, donning free couture dresses, and setting fashion trends.

She went on to star in numerous musical revues in Paris over the next decade. In Europe, her dark skin color opened doors that were closed to her in the United States. In 1927 she married her third husband, manager Count Pepito Abatino, and established herself as a film star and vocalist. In 1930, the song "J'ai Deux Amours" ("I have two loves, my country and Paris") became her signature, and regularly moved Parisians to tears. She increased her international appeal, starring in two films, *Zou Zou* (1934) and *Princesse Tam-Tam* (1935).

Capitalizing on her international fame, Baker returned to New York in 1936, playing to packed houses as the star of the Ziegfeld Follies. Later that year, she opened Chez Josy Baker, a successful nightclub in Manhattan. Reviews of her performances, however, were often racist. Unwilling to tolerate this and other racial inequalities in the United States, she closed Josy's after just one year and became a French citizen, in 1937. During World War II, she served as an intelligence officer, an ambulance driver, and an entertainer with the Free French Air Force in North Africa, earning the prestigious Croix de Guerre and Legion of Honor for her war efforts.

Although she frequently reinvented herself and returned to the stage, she devoted most of her post-war efforts to raising her twelve adopted children of diverse nationalities at Les Milandes, an ideal community of her own creation. She fought racism worldwide and joined Dr. Martin Luther King Jr. in his 1963 March on Washington, her first U.S. appearance in twenty-five years. She married unsuccessfully two more times, but she found comfort in her brood of adoptees, whose education and upbringing ultimately bankrupted her. Close friends, including Princess Grace of Monaco, came to her assistance, and although in ill health most of the last decade of her life, she eventually reestablished herself with comeback performances in New York at Carnegie Hall and the Palace Theater in 1973.

In early April 1975, Baker opened and starred in a show celebrating her fifty years in show business at the Bobino Théâtre in Paris. As she had done on many earlier occasions, she mesmerized her audience, and her adopted city embraced her triumphant return. Only four days after the show's opening, she suffered a massive stroke, and she died in her sleep of a cerebral hemorrhage two days later, April 12, at Salpêtrière Hospital on the eastern edge of Paris. None of Baker's children was with her when she died. One was abroad and the rest were in Monaco.

BEST KNOWN FOR: Her risqué, banana-clad performances at the
                   Folies-Bergère
FIRST JOB: Live-in maid at the age of seven
AVOCATION: Creating a utopian community

RITES OF PASSAGE

Josephine's Baker final performance—her funeral—drew an enormous crowd of devoted fans. Baker's final send-off had all the trappings of a national funeral for a head of state, including a 21-gun salute (the first ever for an American-born Parisian). The fifteen hundred seats in Paris's neoclassical Church of the Madeleine were filled well in advance of the ceremony, although the highest dignitaries were represented by proxies. The entire funeral was broadcast live on state television.

PAYING RESPECTS

On Tuesday, April 15, 1975, Baker's adoring Parisian public came out in droves to pay their respects to "La Baker." Accompanied by a police escort, the cortege left Salpêtrière Hospital for the Church of the Madeleine, passing the Bobino Théâtre, which displayed the word "JOSEPHINE" on the marquee. With police motorcycles clearing a path for the procession, fans threw bouquets of flowers onto the cortege as it traveled.

THE FUNERAL

At the church, Baker's flower-covered casket was adorned with the decorations she had received as Lt. Josephine Baker during World War II. As she had requested before her death, Baker's casket was closed and her sister ensured that she wore no make-up. An enormous cross made of lilacs and roses covered the bier, which was surrounded by a double row of France's tricolor flags. A solitary American flag completed the scene. Seated nearby were Princess Grace and actress Sophia Loren; the French State Secretary for Cultural Affairs; and representatives of the military, including Général Alain de Boissieu, commander of the French Legion of Honor and son-in-law of former president Charles de Gaulle. Mourners filled the church and covered its steps down into the Rue Royale; police officers had to lock arms to restrain the crowds, who filled the streets all the way to the Place de la Concorde, more than a quarter of a mile away.

THE SERVICES   The religious service was respectful and solemn. Harpist Pierre Spiers played a lilting rendition of "Sonny Boy," followed by Baker's signature melody, "J'ai Deux Amours."

A second service for Josephine Baker was held in Monaco on April 19, 1975, at St. Charles Church, where two thousand ardent admirers came to say farewell. Monaco's Princess Grace arranged for the service, which was attended by Baker's children, her sister, and her estranged fourth husband, whom she never divorced, Jo Bouillon.

FINAL RESTING PLACE   Josephine Baker was buried in the Cimetière de Monaco overlooking the Mediterranean Sea. When her husband died in 1984, he was buried with her.

NEWS OF THE DAY
APRIL 12, 1975
LAST AMERICANS LEAVE CAMBODIA; EMBASSY CLOSED

CONGRESS RESISTS U.S. AID IN EVACUATING VIETNAMESE

ONASSIS SAID TO HAVE PLANNED DIVORCE, PROVIDED $3-MILLION FOR WIDOW IN WILL

BEYOND THE GRAVE
ODD COINCIDENCES
Josephine Baker died in the same hospital in Paris where Princess Diana would die twenty-two years later.

Baker's birth date, June 3, was also the burial date of both Ayatollah Khomeini and Pope John XXIII, and she shared her date of death, April 12, and her date of burial, April 15, with Franklin Roosevelt.

MEMORIALS AND TRIBUTES
On November 7, 1976, the Variety Club Foundation of New York City, whose honorary chairs were Princess Grace of Monaco and Jacqueline Onassis, produced a special tribute to Josephine Baker at the Metropolitan Opera in New York.

FANS LOOK ON AS **JOSEPHINE BAKER**'S HEARSE
PASSES THE BOBINO THÉÂTRE IN PARIS'S MONTPARNASSE QUARTER.

SARAH BERNHARDT

"The Divine Sarah"

October 22, 1844–March 26, 1923

"Quand même." ("No matter what.")

FRANCE'S GREATEST ACTRESS TAKES HER FINAL BOW IN HER CUSTOM-MADE, ROSE-WOOD COFFIN.

VITAL STATISTICS

AGE AT DEATH: 78

CAUSE OF DEATH: Uremic poisoning

SURVIVORS: A son, Maurice; two granddaughters, Mme Louis Verneuill and Mme Collin du Bocage; and a great-grandson, M. Grosse

CLOSE CALLS: After an April 1917 kidney operation at Mt. Sinai Hospital in New York, the actress was listed in critical condition, but she recovered.

LAST WORDS: In her final moments, the actress was reported to inquire if the press were waiting on the street to learn news of her. When told that they were, she said, "Then I'll keep them waiting. They tortured me all my life. Now it's my turn to torture them."

HER LIFE

Sarah Bernhardt was arguably the world's first superstar. The beautiful, dark-eyed French actress was born Henriette Rosine Bernard in 1844, only a few years after her countryman Louis J. M. Daguerre invented copper-plate photography. Bernhardt, who reached the pinnacle of her fame in her late thirties, became one of the first performers to successfully use mass photographic reproduction of her image to feed a growing personality cult.

Bernhardt's Dutch-born mother was of Jewish descent; her absentee father was French Catholic. Her mother was a successful courtesan and occasional seamstress and, rather than follow in her mother's footsteps, young Sarah studied acting, beginning in 1860 at the Paris Conservatoire. The impression she made was unremarkable, however, and a short-term contract earned at the Comédie Française was not renewed. Between acting jobs Bernhardt busied herself with romance. When in need, she seemed always to have a gentleman nearby ready to assist her. By 1866 her career picked up, and she was performing regularly at the Odéon Théâtre in modern plays by George Sand, Victor Hugo, and Alexandre Dumas fils, as well as classic works by Shakespeare, Racine, and Molière.

The Franco-Prussian War of 1870–71 interrupted her acting work, and she became a nurse. Transforming the Odéon into a hospital, she earned a place in the hearts of many Parisians for her selfless charity when the city was under siege. When she was able to return to acting, again at the Comédie Française in 1872, she was a beloved and rising star.

Strong-headed and argumentative, Bernhardt clashed frequently with the management of the Comédie Française over her assigned roles, and she once stormed out of the venerable theater after the troupe's director fined her for riding in a hot-air balloon on the day of a performance. When the Divine Sarah finally broke her lifetime contract with the company, in 1880, a French court forced her to pay the company 100,000 francs in lost revenue; Bernhardt never looked back.

Upon severing her contacts with the Comédie Française, Bernhardt formed her own theater company. She closed every performance at her theater by leading the audience in singing the French national anthem, returning to the stage three and four times to lead the standing patrons who joined with her golden voice, tears streaming down their faces.

In November 1880, she headed for the United States for the first time, where she performed at Booth's Theater in New York City, one of 27 performances in Manhattan. Acting in scenes from eight different dramas, including *La*

Dame aux Camélias by Dumas fils, Bernhardt proceeded to tour fifty more cities, giving 156 additional performances. Bernhardt made nine different tours of the United States from 1881 to 1917, performing in small theaters on the vaudeville circuit. The nature and style of her acting, always in French, transcended language. The great tragedienne's scenes were violent or emotive, leaving no question as to their meaning. Her broad and gestural style of acting—pantomimes of fear, joy, surprise, anger, and understanding—which now would seem cliché, was in fact a pioneering technique soon imitated by silent-film actors and an exciting departure from the staid acting conventions of the nineteenth century. Her revolutionary acting style, even in Shakespeare's *Hamlet,* would reverberate throughout the twentieth century—her whisper of Hamlet's soliloquy transformed later interpretations of the tragic hero.

The eccentric Bernhardt, beloved in five continents, abhorred ocean voyages and yet made a number of them, always traveling with a rosewood coffin made to her specifications. To encourage interest in Bernhardt's appearances before her arrival in a town, promoters would send many of her personal belongings ahead for display, invariably including the coffin and photos of the actress walking her two pet leopards.

Despite a lifetime of illnesses, including kidney ailments, sciatica, and inflammation of the knee (which led to the eventual amputation of her right leg in 1915), the actress displayed enormous energy, making grueling tours across several continents, performing for French troops on the battle lines of World War I, and making the patriotic film *Mothers of France* while at the front. Almost fifty years after she nursed the wounded at the Odéon, she turned her Théâtre Sarah Bernhardt into a hospital to treat the casualties of the Great War.

The French actress made and spent several fortunes, often giving generously to charitable causes, which further endeared her to her countrymen. She chose to lead what she referred to in her memoirs as *"ma double vie"* ("my double life"). Catholic and Jewish, single and married, performing as a man or woman, she led a dual life in her brilliant and wide-ranging performances onstage, and her personal affairs offstage.

Bernhardt's life was full of contradictions. In 1882, she married an actor, Jacques Demala, only to divorce him after one year, but then to nurse him seven years later when he was on his deathbed. She bore one child, Maurice, whose father she clearly loved but did not marry. She was tired and ill at the end of her life, yet she was acting in an American film, playing a paralytic, when she died. She was vain yet selfless in her love of her family and her country. Despite the innumerable global honors she received for her acting, winning the Cross of the Legion of Honor was her proudest achievement. She became an officer in February 1922, the first in the theatrical profession to receive France's highest honor.

When Bernhardt took ill in March 1923, the state of her health became international news. The *New York Times* ran front-page updates for two days before her death. On March 26, 1923, as it became clear that the actress would not survive the night, family members called in Bernhardt's loyal staff, who made tearful farewells. Doctors called a priest, who performed the sacrament of extreme unction. Too weak to respond verbally, Bernhardt indicated her understanding of the prayers with her expressive, dark brown eyes. With her family and doctors nearby, the legend of the international stage died in the arms of her son Maurice at 7:59 P.M. in her Paris home.

BEST KNOWN FOR: Her unforgettable stage presence, celebrity, and voice

FIRST JOB: Courtesan in her mother's establishment

AVOCATIONS: Sculpting and writing

ORPHANS FLANK THE HORSE-DRAWN HEARSE CARRYING
THE BODY OF **SARAH BERNHARDT** AS CROWDS PACK THE
ROUTE TO PÈRE LACHAISE CEMETERY IN PARIS.

RITES OF PASSAGE

Although Parisians anticipated the death of their most celebrated citizen, its reality hit hard. The news of the great tragedienne's death was signified by the lowering of the curtain at the Théâtre Sarah Bernhardt before the end of the first act of one of her signature plays, *L'Aiglon*. When management shared the sad news with the audience, the people left, devastated, keeping their ticket stubs as mementos of her death.

THE PREPARATION

Bernhardt had long expressed a desire to be buried on Belle-Isle-en-Mer, where she had readied a tomb carved in the rocky hillside, but newspapers reported that Bernhardt had been forced to sell her home there and had died penniless. The government offered to pay the cost of Bernhardt's farewell and suggested a national funeral beginning at either the Church of the Madeleine or Notre Dame Cathedral. Maurice Bernhardt refused, saying that his mother had wished a simple service and a mass at her neighborhood church. Even so, learning of Bernhardt's financial circumstances, city officials insisted on paying the bill for the burial.

PAYING RESPECTS

Hundreds of fans waited in vigil outside Bernhardt's home. On Tuesday, March 27, they were permitted to view the body. Silently, with many of them bearing bouquets, they filed through the entrance hallway (where the words "Quand même" were emblazoned on the walls), up the stairs, past photographic mementos, through the actress's boudoir, and finally into her bedchamber where, laid out in white satin and covered with a white tulle veil, Bernhardt rested.

The next day, Bernhardt's body lay in the rosewood coffin she had had designed more than thirty years earlier and had toted with her ever since.

Pinned to her chest was the Cross of the Legion of Honor, her crowning achievement. Around her neck hung the locket she always wore, containing a portrait of her son and a lock of his hair.

The family improvised a "chapel" in a downstairs parlor to receive mourners, with the walls draped in black and a bier, covered in a silver-fringed black pall, holding the coffin. Knowing that his mother adored flowers, Maurice Bernhardt ensured that the small room was filled with floral tributes. The family said prayers for their beloved at eleven o'clock. At noon, they opened the parlor to members of the public who, on their lunch hour, came to say good-bye.

THE FUNERAL

Bernhardt's death occurred during the Christian Holy Week, the solemn seven days that culminate on Easter Sunday. The actress's funeral took place on Holy Thursday, the day before Good Friday. Crowds gathered on the morning of Thursday, March 29, outside Bernhardt's home and along the route to the Church of Saint François de Sales. At half past six, Bernhardt's family once more opened the doors to the actress's home to mourners until eight o'clock, when a hearse arrived to bear her body to the funeral.

At the church, four rows of candles surrounded the catafalque where the actress lay. The nave and entry to the church were draped in heavy black bunting trimmed with silver fringe that spelled the actress's initials, "S. B." Two registries met visitors entering the church, which overflowed with flowers.

The mobs on the adjoining streets—Boulevard Malesherbes and Rue Ampere—straining for a glimpse of the body of France's most celebrated personality, could not be contained. By ten o'clock in the morning the police had called for reinforcements, and the Republican Guard arrived to assist them. Journalists of the day compared the throng to that at the funeral of Victor Hugo, and to the "Victory Parade" of July 14, 1919, which marked the end of the World War I.

THE SERVICE In exception to Holy Week prohibitions, choral music was allowed. Grieg's "La Mort D'Aase" accompanied the processional, followed by a recitation of the De Profundis and Vespers of the Dead. Noted singer Mme Reynard sang Fauré's "Pie Jesu" and M. Narcon of the Paris Opera sang "Liberanos" by Samuel Rousseau. Fauré's "In Paradisum" and Gluck's "Chant Funebre" followed, and a Beethoven symphony (conflicting accounts claim the Third and the Seventh) accompanied the recessional.

Coinciding with the Paris tribute, on the tiny island of Belle-Isle-en-Mer, off the Brittany coast, where Bernhardt had spent many summer holidays, villagers gathered in a solemn ceremony that the great actress would have loved: fishermen and townsfolk, walking in silence, threw flowers across a drawbridge at the edge of an ocean precipice.

THE PROCESSION With the streets outside the church nearly impassable, French gendarmes and reinforcements from the army strained to contain onlookers during the solemn procession to the cemetery. At least a million people lined the wide boulevards between the Church of the Madeleine and the Théâtre Sarah Bernhardt. The cortege stopped in front of the theater while a wreath was taken from the hearse and placed on the door of the actress's dressing room.

The wagon bearing Bernhardt's coffin was blanketed in her favorite flowers: lilies, violets, roses, and lilacs. In response to Bernhardt's son's request, mourners had sent so many floral tributes that six wagons, overloaded with spring blooms, followed the hearse. Orphan girls, each carrying a palm

frond, walked alongside the actress's car. Mourners followed the cortege on foot; several fainted, and others were crushed while straining to glimpse Bernhardt's coffin.

FINAL RESTING PLACE The five-mile journey across Paris to Père Lachaise cemetery, where crowds of mourners were in attendance, took three hours. With no eulogy, Sarah Bernhardt's coffin was placed, with a gold crucifix, into the black marble mausoleum where her mother was buried.

After the graveside service, Maurice Bernhardt and his son-in-law, playwright Louis Verneuill, along with Mme Bernhardt's closest friend, painter Louise Abema, shook hands with mourners, thanking them for their condolences. Thousands filed through lines of policemen, many adding single flowers to the mountain of blooms heaped before the Divine Sarah's tomb.

NEWS OF THE DAY
MARCH 27, 1923
BERNHARDT DIES IN HER SON'S ARMS IN PARIS, AGED 78

SOVIET COURT DOOMS ARCHBISHOP TO DIE

AROUND THE WORLD
The U.S. vaudeville theaters owned by Keith, Proctor, and Moss staged a memorial tribute to Bernhardt at each of their circuit theaters at 3:00 P.M. on March 29. This vaudeville circuit was the last to have hosted Sarah Bernhardt on her 1917 farewell tour of the country. All shows were halted and bells rang out seventy-eight times, one for each year of the actress's life.

BEYOND THE GRAVE

Sarah Bernhardt was always prepared for her own death, carrying a rosewood coffin with her wherever she traveled, but she might as well have left it at home. Finally, thirty years after construction, it was pressed into service; the familiar prop was in her bedroom, where she died.

Bernhardt's world-famous menagerie, including a panther, two leopards, a dozen dogs, and two alligators, was slowly sold off in her last year to help pay the actress's debts. At her death, her collection was down to ten dogs and a single parrot, which, perching nearby, watched silently as crowds passed the actress's bed. The day after the funeral, the dogs and bird were put up for sale.

SECRETS TO THE GRAVE

The ever-dramatic Bernhardt never revealed the name of her son's father. Despite this, Bernhardt considered him to be one of the great loves of her life. Post-mortem sleuthing has identified him as Henri, Prince de Ligne of Belgium, whose family wished to avoid scandal.

LAST WISHES

Bernhardt asked for no eulogies at her funeral: "I want flowers, not a crown."

WINSTON CHURCHILL

"Old Warrior"

November 30, 1874–January 24, 1965

"When I get to heaven I mean to spend a considerable portion of my first million years in painting."

WINSTON CHURCHILL'S IMAGE PEERS OUT FROM BLACK-BORDERED NEWSPAPERS ANNOUNCING HIS DEATH, AT LONDON'S PICCADILLY CIRCUS.

VITAL STATISTICS

AGE AT DEATH: 90

CAUSE OF DEATH: Multiple strokes

SURVIVORS: His wife, Clementine Hozier Churchill; two daughters, Lady Christopher Soames and Sarah; and a son, Randolph

CLOSE CALLS: In 1931, Churchill was hit by a car and seriously injured crossing Fifth Avenue in New York City while on a lecture tour. Ten years later, soon after the United States entered World War II, Churchill had a heart attack at the White House after meeting with President Franklin D. Roosevelt; this fact was kept quiet by officials in England and the United States in an effort to maintain the public's confidence in the Allied war effort.

LAST WORDS: "I'm so bored with it all."

HIS LIFE

The son of Lord Randolph Churchill, a descendant of the first Duke of Marlborough, and American Jennie Jerome, Winston Leonard Spencer Churchill made a grand entrance into British aristocracy, born, literally, at Blenheim Palace. Although he was only an average student, Churchill distinguished himself early as a skillful orator. Later, at the Royal Military Academy at Sandhurst, Churchill excelled in his study of military tactics, which would subsequently influence his political strategy for Great Britain during World War II. As a young officer observing the war between Spain and the United States in Cuba in 1895, Churchill began to write about his military adventures. In South Africa during the Boer War in 1897, Churchill wrote a firsthand account of a military unit's capture and incarceration, and his own jailbreak, an escapade that won him instant notoriety and acclaim as a hero back home.

Always the political animal, Sir Winston changed party affiliations more than once during his career. In 1900 he was first elected to Parliament as a member of the Conservative Party. Churchill suffered political and military setbacks early on, notably Britain's naval loss in the Dardanelles (1915), a loss for which, as First Lord of the Admiralty, he was responsible. Churchill later switched to the Liberal Party. During that time he remained active in world affairs by giving speeches, writing essays, and developing policies. Churchill held several cabinet-level positions from 1917 to 1922, and from 1924 to 1929 he served in the House of Commons, as a Conservative, joining Neville Chamberlain's Conservative Party when it took power in the 1930s. In particular, he was a harbinger of Germany's impending threat. Sensing a need for alliance, Chamberlain offered Churchill his previously held cabinet position of Lord of the Admiralty, which Churchill accepted. Later that year he succeeded Chamberlain as prime minister at age sixty-five, an age when most Britons are set for retirement. Churchill led England during the country's most stressful war years, from 1940 to 1945, and later returned for a second turn as prime minister from 1951 to 1955. His parliamentary career spanned sixty years.

Churchill's ability as a speaker of great eloquence reached its apogee during World War II. His radio oratories strengthened the resolve of Allied soldiers in the field and encouraged U.S. involvement in the war effort. His intrepid stand against the enemy, as London was bombarded by Nazi warplanes, embodied the moral force that confronted and overcame Hitler's despotism.

Churchill suffered from fatigue, pneumonia, a bad heart, a nagging eye irritation, and deafness even before his final retirement from public life in 1955 at the age of eighty-one. When he suffered several strokes and his condition deteriorated further, his family prepared plans for his funeral. In 1958, they adopted the plan code-named "Hope Not"; seven years later it would be realized in the exalted pageantry of his funeral. Churchill's funeral was the British Broadcasting Corporation's (BBC) most intricate production to date. In anticipation of this huge media event, the BBC had set television cables in the floor of Westminster Abbey a full two years before Churchill's death.

BEST KNOWN FOR: His tireless and impassioned opposition to Hitler and the Third Reich

FIRST JOB: Military officer and journalist

AVOCATIONS: Painting, writing, bricklaying, and horse breeding

RITES OF PASSAGE

THE FUNERAL

On Saturday, January 30, 1965, an estimated 350 million viewers worldwide were riveted by the solemn ceremonies of Churchill's funeral, which were televised live by a then-groundbreaking satellite relay. Commentators included former U.S. president Dwight Eisenhower for the BBC and actors Sir Laurence Olivier and Paul Scofield for the competing Independent Television Authority (ITA) network.

The magnitude of the feeling for Churchill was likewise expressed in the print media. Hundreds of daily, weekly, and monthly journals provided minute details of the Old Warrior's funeral ceremonies. Even seven months after Churchill was laid to rest, *National Geographic* devoted the majority of its August 1965 issue to his funeral. The issue contained a specially constructed vinyl record, *Sir Winston Churchill's Funeral,* narrated by news correspondent David Brinkley.

Breaking with royal tradition, Queen Elizabeth requested that the House of Commons provide a special state funeral for Churchill, a commoner, stating, "My people . . . should have an opportunity of expressing their sorrow at the loss and their veneration of the memory of that outstanding man who in war and peace served his country unfailingly for more than fifty years and in the hours of our greatest danger was the inspiring leader who strengthened and supported us all."

She also authorized that the Right Honorable Sir Winston Churchill, Knight of the Garter (K.G.) lay in state at Westminster Abbey, and she herself came to pay her respects, the first reigning monarch to honor a commoner. The Queen stood among three hundred thousand mourners paying silent tribute to Churchill, who lay in a Union Jack–draped coffin set atop a seven-foot-high catafalque. Later, she would again breach royal tradition to attend his funeral.

THE PROCESSION At 9:15 AM, the bells of Big Ben chimed before being silenced for the day. A single cannon shot marked the beginning of the cortege, which crept from London's Westminster Abbey, where Sir Winston had lain in state, to St. Paul's Cathedral for the service. From there, it proceeded to the Tower Pier, where Churchill's remains sailed a final time up the Thames River to Festival Hall, on the opposite embankment.

The route passed the monuments that had been important in Winston Churchill's life—Parliament Square; Whitehall Palace; 10 Downing Street, the prime minister's residence; the Admiralty, where he held his first cabinet job; Fleet Street, in remembrance of his days as a journalist; the Cenotaph memorial to the British dead of both world wars—before arriving for obsequies at St. Paul's Cathedral and then his water-borne farewell from the Tower of London.

On the day of the funeral millions of Britons lined the streets, many of them having spent the night out in the wintry, damp London air to ensure their view of the procession, a small sacrifice for the man whom many credited with saving them from Hitler's tyranny. Veterans wearing their wartime medals wept openly for the leader who had inspired their courage through the Blitz and horrors of war.

The cortege stretched more than one mile. Heralds wearing medieval and Tudor costumes, in silks and brocades, that bore the emblems of Churchill's family; Irish hussars; Scottish pipers; military bands; banner bearers; guardsmen; and delegates from the military, police, and fire services were among the more than forty groups marching in the procession. Sailors of the Royal Navy, numbering 142, pulled the gun carriage bearing Churchill's five-hundred-pound lead coffin. Queen Elizabeth's own town coach transported Churchill's wife, Clementine, and their two daughters, while the male family members walked directly behind the gun carriage.

THE SERVICE Under the dome of the great St. Paul's Cathedral lay England's great warrior, a most fitting tribute, since the cavernous cathedral had survived the London Blitz when Churchill served as prime minister. In contrast to the solemnity of Handel's "Dead March," which had accompanied the procession outside, inspirational music marked the services inside the cathedral. The congregation sang several hymns, including "The Battle Hymn of the Republic," which had been chosen by Churchill himself in the early plans for his funeral out of respect for his mother's American lineage. A solo trumpeter in medieval dress played "Last Post," to which a hussar in military uniform responded with "Reveille."

Twelve honorary pallbearers escorted the casket from St. Paul's, where the gun carriage and cortege waited to continue the funeral march to the Tower of London and then to the launch on the Thames River. At the pier Scottish and Irish pipers played dirges while Churchill's coffin was placed on the river launch *Havengore,* headed for Festival Hall.

FINAL RESTING PLACE As the launch passed below, the imposing dock cranes of the Thames bowed in respect. A band on shore played "Rule Britannia," followed by a nineteen-gun salute, and then four groups of four Royal Air Force jets flew in formation above the launch as Churchill's body left London for the last time. When the launch arrived at Festival Hall, a plain hearse carried his remains to Waterloo Station, where they were placed on a train pulled by steam locomotive 34051, known for some time as the "Winston Churchill," bound for his family's burial site in Bladon churchyard.

After a five-minute private graveside service from which the media were politely but firmly asked to remain away, Winston Churchill was laid to rest alongside his mother and father.

NEWS OF THE DAY
JANUARY 24, 1965
CHURCHILL DIES AT 90 AT HOME IN LONDON

PRESIDENT IS ILL;
GOES TO HOSPITAL WITH BAD COUGH

MONKS IN VIETNAM ASSAIL U.S. ENVOY;
LIBRARY IS RAIDED

JANUARY 25, 1965

**DE GAULLE IN TRIBUTE
TO COMRADE IN ARMS
AS "GREATEST" OF ERA**

NEW MATH IS REPLACING THIRD "R"

AROUND THE WORLD

In New York City, the 234-year-old Liberty Bell at the Middle Collegiate Reformed Church at Second Avenue and Seventh Street rang ninety-one times, once for each year of Churchill's life with a final toll in respect. The same Liberty Bell had rung in 1776 for the signing of the Declaration of Independence and has rung thereafter at every inauguration and death of an American president. Nationwide, the American flag was lowered to half-mast for a week in honor of the fallen British leader.

BEYOND THE GRAVE

In the 1920s, unsure of his talent, Churchill painted and sold his work under the pseudonym "Charles Morin." In 1947, two of his paintings were accepted into the Royal Academy under the name "Mr. Winter." After his death, Churchill's oil paintings became prized collectibles.

Churchill won the Nobel Prize in literature in 1953 for his masterpiece, *The Second World War,* his personal narrative of the war in six volumes.

ODD COINCIDENCES

Sir Winston Churchill and his father, Lord Randolph Churchill, both passed away on the same date, seventy years apart.

Winston Churchill was buried on what would have been the eighty-third birthday of his most important ally, President Franklin D. Roosevelt. As bells tolled in London, nearly sixty people gathered at FDR's grave in Hyde Park, New York, to remember the great American leader.

~ A HANDWRITTEN NOTE FROM ELIZABETH II, QUEEN OF ENGLAND, ON A FLORAL ARRANGEMENT AT THE CEMETERY WHERE **CHURCHILL** IS BURIED.

~ THE MIGHTY CRANES ON THE THAMES ARE POSED TO BOW AS THE LAUNCH BEARING **CHURCHILL**'S COFFIN PASSES BENEATH THEM.

SALVADOR DALÍ

"Avida Dollars"

May 11, 1904–January 23, 1989

"The difference between a madman and me is that I am not mad."

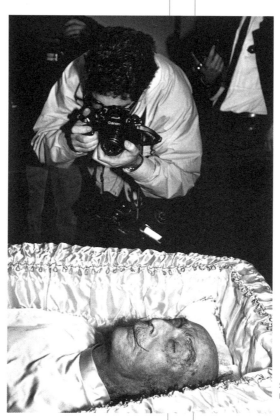

A PHOTOGRAPHER ZEROES IN ON THE SPANISH SURREALIST AS HE LIES IN STATE AT HIS GALATEA TOWER HOME.

↝ **DALÍ**'S BLACK-LACQUERED COFFIN
ITS PLACE OF HONOR IN THE CENTER OF TH
TEATRO-MUSEO DALÍ, BENEATH AN ENORMO
WIFE, GALA.

FINAL RESTING PLACE Four museum guards wearing gold and blue carried the artist's black-lacquered casket from the church across a square bearing the artist's name. As the pallbearers entered the arched doorway of the egg-spired, bread-sculpture-encrusted Teatro-Museo Dalí, thousands of onlookers applauded. The coffin was lowered into a marble hole in the floor centered beneath a geodesic cupola. Embalmers claimed that Dalí's body would last three hundred years.

Above Dalí's tomb hung an enormous, wall-size painting of his nude wife, Gala, entitled *Lincoln in Dalí Vision* because from a distance the body of his wife transforms into a portrait of Abraham Lincoln. As planned, his coffin passed a sculpture entitled *Cobla,* which depicted a band of musicians, while nearby was another famous Dalí work, his 1938 sculpture *Rainy Taxi,* featuring a real Cadillac with a coin-operated mechanism that causes rain on the inside of the automobile.

NEWS OF THE DAY
JANUARY 24, 1989

SOVIETS REPORT 1,000 DEAD IN QUAKE-INDUCED SLIDE

CENTRAL ASIA VILLAGES BURIED IN HUGE FLOW OF STONE AND MUD

IN THIRD WORLD, THE LEGACY OF MARX TAKES MANY SHAPES

SALVADOR DALÍ, PIONEER SURREALIST, DIES AT 84

AROUND THE WORLD

Nearby, across the French border, the mayor of Perpignan renamed the square in front of the train station "Place Salvador Dalí" because the surrealist had once referred to it as "the cosmic navel of the world."

BEYOND THE GRAVE

Dalí left his estate, valued at nearly $90 million, to the Spanish government, in an affront to his province of Catalonia, which had anticipated being the recipient of his legacy. Dalí remembered neither his caretakers nor his close friends in his will.

The value of the fake art created on the blank paper signed by Dalí was estimated at the time of his death to be in excess of $700 million.

THOMAS EDISON

"The Wizard of Menlo Park"

February 11, 1847–October 18, 1931

"There is no substitute for hard work."

〰 "THE WIZARD OF MENLO PARK," RIGHT,
SHAKES HANDS WITH GOOD FRIEND HENRY FORD
ON **EDISON**'S EIGHTIETH BIRTHDAY.

VITAL STATISTICS

AGE AT DEATH: 84

CAUSE OF DEATH: Heart failure

SURVIVORS: His wife, Mina Edison; their three children, Mrs. John Eyre Sloane, Charles, and Theodore; and three children from his first marriage, Thomas Jr., William, and Mrs. Marion Oser

LAST WORDS: "It's very beautiful over there."

HIS LIFE

Few men have affected modern life as dramatically as did Thomas Alva Edison, whose life and work spanned two centuries and whose inventions made an indelible imprint on life in the twentieth century.

The "benefactor of all humanity," as President Herbert Hoover once referred to Edison, was born in humble but not poor surroundings in Milan, Ohio, the last of seven children of Samuel and Nancy Elliott Edison. His father, a successful business owner, moved the family to Port Huron, Michigan, when young Thomas was seven. Edison was a poor student, possibly suffering from learning disorders, so his mother chose to teach him at home after he completed only three years of formal schooling. He was and would always be an avid reader. Eschewing math, he excelled in chemistry, and at age ten he built his first laboratory at home. At fifteen, Edison, who was hearing impaired, taught himself Morse code, later becoming a telegraph operator.

He spent his teen years as an itinerant worker on the railroads, stopping also to work at various telegraph offices. In 1868, at age twenty-one, Edison took a job at the Western Union Telegraph Company in Boston. That year he also patented his first invention, a machine to record votes, a commercial failure that nevertheless opened his eyes to the value of inventing useful products. He made connections in the financial industry after making improvements to stock ticker-tape machines and soon moved to New York City.

Although he sometimes skated on thin financial ice, Edison always found his way to solid ground through ingenuity and opportunity. In 1869, he formed a partnership of electrical engineers, at that time a new profession, and when competitors bought out the firm a year later, Edison used the capital to start a company focusing on practical inventions.

In the 1870s Edison, with his fifty employees, improved the telegraph as well as modifying the inventions of others, dissecting them and making adjustments large and small. In 1876 he moved his laboratory to Menlo Park, New Jersey, and it was here in 1878 that he invented his favorite machine, the phonograph, as well as the incandescent lightbulb a year later, among numerous other electrical innovations, earning him the nickname "The Wizard of Menlo Park."

Edison married his first wife, Mary, on Christmas Day in 1871, and the couple had two sons and a daughter. During their marriage, Edison worked slavishly at his lab, often not returning to his home for several days at a time. "Genius," Edison famously said, "is one percent inspiration and ninety-nine percent perspiration." Mary died in 1884. Two years later, just shy of his fortieth birthday, Edison married his second wife, Mina Miller, whose wealthy father funded some of his son-in-law's work and bailed him out when projects failed.

In 1887, the inventor built a larger lab to accommodate his experiments in West Orange, New Jersey, close to the brick Victorian house on fifteen acres he shared with his new wife in Llewelyn Park. More than half of Edison's 1,093 patents were registered after the move, including the fluoroscope, improvements to movie industry technology, and methods of iron extraction and cement manufacture. The lab would eventually employ ten thousand people. But perhaps his greatest creation was the concept of a private research, development, and production laboratory in which teams of engineers worked on multiple projects, a now-common approach to technological problem solving.

Like his good friend and fellow innovator Henry Ford, Edison aimed to produce inexpensive, mass-produced objects that would be useful in daily life, less interested in the magic of an invention than in the reality of its applications. He often completely lost interest in his inventions once he'd worked out the kinks and found a commercial use for them (often establishing companies to promote them, which he sometimes named after himself). He left the business responsibilities related to his patents to others, but he made sure to hire the best possible attorneys to protect his patents.

Edison's projects at the beginning of the twentieth century included the mimeograph, a dictation machine, a storage battery, and railway lighting improvements. The advent of World War I led him to military applications and inventions, and he received the Distinguished Service Medal in 1920 for his work on periscopes and torpedo devices. Voted "the greatest living American" in a 1922 *New York Times* poll, Edison busied himself in his later years traveling to deliver speeches and receive awards, reducing his time in the lab. He retired from the Thomas Alva Edison Company in 1926, leaving his son Charles in charge, and the following year on his eightieth birthday he founded a new company to investigate inexpensive substitutes for rubber, at the request of friends Harvey Firestone and Henry Ford. In 1928 Edison received the country's highest honor, a gold Congressional Medal, which he

accepted from West Orange via a radio hookup with President Calvin Coolidge in Washington, D.C.

In 1929, at a huge celebration to mark the fiftieth anniversary of Edison's incandescent lightbulb hosted by Henry Ford in Michigan, Edison collapsed. The eighty-two-year-old inventor's subsequent recovery was darkened by two years of illness, including a diagnosis of Bright's disease (kidney inflammation) and stomach ulcers, and later uremia. He fell into a coma a week before he died, from which he emerged intermittently. Knowing that Edison's death was drawing near, his family installed eight telephones in his Llewelyn Park, New Jersey, home, staffed by operators ready to dial President Herbert Hoover, Harvey Firestone, Henry Ford, and others at a moment's notice. Edison finally succumbed at 3:24 A.M. on Sunday, October 18, 1931, with his wife, Mina, at his side.

BEST KNOWN FOR: The lightbulb
FIRST JOB: Self-employed food-and-newspaper salesman on railroad cars
AVOCATION: Reading

RITES OF PASSAGE

Beginning on Sunday, October 18, 1931, the *New York Times* ran front-page stories on Edison's death for five consecutive days, each with a full page of tributes from dignitaries, world leaders, and captains of industry. Albert Einstein said of Edison, "An inventive spirit has filled his own life and all our existence with bright light."

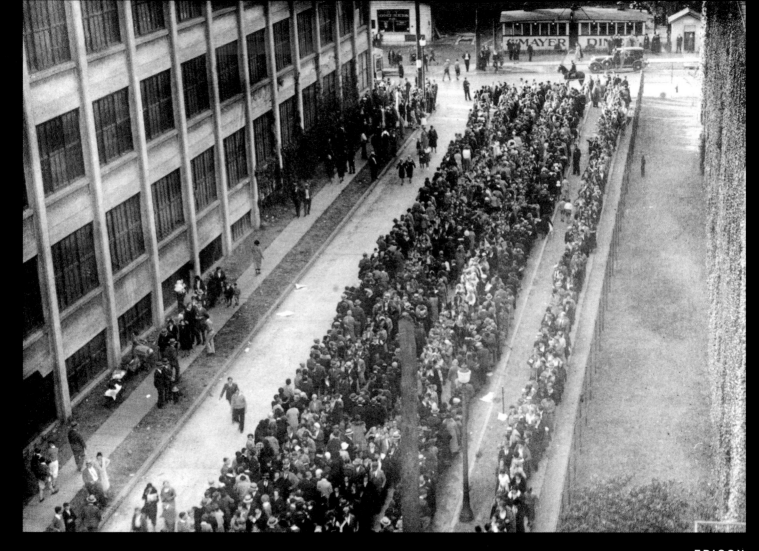

CROWDS WAIT ON LINE OUTSIDE **EDISON**'S WEST
ORANGE LAB WHERE HIS BODY LAY IN STATE.

THE INVENTOR'S COFFIN TAKES CENTER STAGE IN THE
EDISON LABORATORY LIBRARY BEFORE PUBLIC VIEWING.

THE PREPARATION

Edison's family kept the funeral, held at the family home, a private affair, but they agreed to allow his body to lie in state for several days in the library of his West Orange laboratory, just a few minutes from his home, to accommodate the grief-stricken public. On Monday, October 19, at 6:45 A.M., Edison's widow and her children accompanied his bronze coffin to the laboratory, where they spent an hour preparing the facility for public viewing. Dressed in his signature wing collar shirt and black string tie, the great inventor's body lay in a glass-covered, open casket with a bronze nameplate engraved with his signature, at one end of the laboratory. White chrysanthemums and a bouquet of claret-colored dahlias, which Mrs. Edison, an avid horticulturist, had developed and named "Thomas Alva Edison," were set near the bier.

Two days later, a sculptor rendered a death mask of Edison shortly before his body was placed in its coffin.

PAYING RESPECTS

At 8:00 A.M. on the first day of public viewing, two thousand of Edison's employees and their families were admitted to pay their respects, and at 9:00 the first of more than ten thousand members of the public filed past Edison's bier, including women with babies, and schoolchildren released from their studies. Long-time Edison employees served as honor guards, and twice that day the Reverend Arthur Brown of the Methodist Church, where Mrs. Edison worshipped, prayed over Edison's body. Although not a member of any formal religion, Edison had said he believed in a "supreme intelligence." That evening, radio station WOR in New York City broadcast a tribute to Edison, featuring speeches, testimonials, and telegrams of tribute.

On Tuesday, October 20, more than forty thousand people passed through the laboratory to view Edison at a rate of two thousand people per hour. His

family opened the viewing early, at 7:00 A.M., and left the lab open until well after midnight. Edison's sons finally retrieved his body at 5:00 A.M. on October 21 to bring it home for the funeral services that afternoon.

Events of the day included the arrival of Harvey Firestone and Henry Ford; the presentation of an American flag by veterans of World War I; and a private viewing for a group of 125 "Edison Pioneers" who had worked with the inventor from the beginning. William H. Meadowcroft, Edison's personal secretary for more than fifty years, recovering from a bout of pneumonia, wept uncontrollably when brought to his boss's coffin.

THE FUNERAL

Three hundred close friends and relatives attended the private funeral at the inventor's home. The home, known as "Glenmont," was decorated by lilies, and a warm coal fire glowed inside. A wreath of lilies from the Edison Pioneers held a note that read, "Farewell, Master." The downstairs parlor holding Edison's closed casket was filled with floral tributes. The immediate family chose to remain in a drawing room upstairs, secluded from the service. In an application of one of Edison's greatest inventions, an amplified sound system and a microphone, hidden in flowers downstairs, carried the service to the family upstairs.

THE SERVICE The service commenced at three o'clock, half an hour late, with two of Edison's favorite songs, "I'll Take You Home Again, Kathleen" and "Little Gray Home in the West," played on the family pipe organ, followed by Bach's "Air," Beethoven's *Moonlight Sonata,* Wagner's "Song to the Evening Star," and Arnesky's "Elegy."

The Reverend Dr. Stephen J. Herben, a family friend and former pastor of the Methodist Episcopal Church in Orange, New Jersey, then read the

Twenty-third Psalm, followed by a prayer. For a eulogy, Dr. Lewis Perry, headmaster of Phillips Exeter Academy, read a tribute to Edison that had been written for the anniversary celebration of the lightbulb, at which Edison had collapsed: "[He has] bestowed upon the human race blessings instead of bondage, service instead of serfdom, construction instead of conquest." The service closed with a reading of a poem, "They Do Not Die," by Alice Marston Seaman.

FINAL RESTING PLACE The funeral cortege took a circuitous route from Glenmont to the Rosedale Cemetery in West Orange in order to avoid the thousands of onlookers lining the streets. Arriving at twilight, the immediate family were accompanied by Mrs. Herbert Hoover, the Henry Fords, and the Harvey Firestones. State troopers kept vigil over the burial site, which was adorned by hundreds of floral arrangements, including huge wreaths from the Hoovers (one of green magnolias and one of orchids, gardenias, lavender, and bouvardia) and from Henry Ford (orchids and goldenrod). The use of goldenrod in Ford's wreath was a reference to Edison's recent success in using the flower's juices to form vulcanized rubber.

After a fifteen-minute service led by Rev. Dr. Stephen Herben, Mrs. Edison kissed her husband's casket and, as it was lowered, threw a single rose into the grave. Edison's six children also tossed flowers into their father's grave. By the end of the ceremony, the sun had set.

That night, President Herbert Hoover requested a nationwide, voluntary blackout for one minute, at 9:59 P.M. eastern time, in memory of the man who invented the electric lightbulb. Although the synchronization was not precise, the coast-to-coast tribute included, in New York City, the shutdown of most of Broadway's lights, the Statue of Liberty's torch, the subways, and film projectors in movie theaters. Earlier in the day, commodity exchanges had stopped trading for one minute at the scheduled time of the funeral, and movie studios had stopped production on both coasts for three minutes, in tribute to the man who had literally invented their profession.

NEWS OF THE DAY

OCTOBER 18, 1931

THOMAS EDISON DIES IN COMA AT 84; FAMILY WITH HIM AS THE END COMES

CAPONE CONVICTED OF DODGING TAXES; MAY GET 17 YEARS

OCTOBER 19, 1931

WORLD MOURNS THE DEATH OF EDISON; BODY TO LIE IN STATE IN LABORATORY

"NAZIS" BATTLE FOES AS HITLER DECLARES HE CAN KEEP ORDER

OTHER DEATHS

John Ott, Edison's friend and loyal employee for more than fifty years, died of shock upon learning of his mentor's death. He was seventy-five. Ott's walking stick, crutches, and wheelchair were placed in tribute at Edison's coffin while it lay in the laboratory, and he was buried near the inventor in Rosedale Cemetery on the day of Edison's funeral.

AROUND THE WORLD

Stories on Edison's death ran for several days on the front pages of newspapers in Paris, London, Berlin, Prague, Rome, and Vienna. Condolences poured in to Edison's family from around the globe, including one from Pope Pius XI.

The municipal council in Paris, France, immediately moved to rename a street "Rue Edison," after the inventor.

BEYOND THE GRAVE

Contractors built Yankee Stadium in 1922 using two hundred thousand bags of cement from one of Edison's companies, the Edison Portland Cement Company.

At the end of his life Edison was totally deaf. As Edison's hearing worsened, his wife used Morse code to tap out their dinner companions' conversation on his knee under the table. The inventor had taught Mrs. Edison the code during their courtship.

In 1999, *Time* magazine named Thomas Alva Edison as its "Man of the Nineteenth Century."

At the request of his son Charles, a former governor of New Jersey, Thomas Edison's body and that of his wife Mina Edison, who died in 1947, were exhumed and reinterred at the family home on April 3, 1963. Their graves lie next to one another on the grounds of the Glenmont estate. Edison's first wife, Mary Stilwell Edison, is buried in Mt. Pleasant Cemetery in Newark, New Jersey.

ODD COINCIDENCES

Thomas Edison was buried on October 21, exactly fifty-two years, to the day, after he invented the electric lightbulb.

Edison's employees reported that the usually reliable clock that dominated his cavernous laboratory stopped at 3:27 A.M., three minutes after the inventor's death.

MEMORIALS AND TRIBUTES

The U.S. National Park Service maintains Edison's West Orange laboratory and his home, Glenmont, as a single National Historic Site, housing more than four hundred thousand artifacts, including all his notebooks, business correspondence, employees' notes, family papers, media exchanges, and letters from the public.

Edison's Menlo Park laboratory, which Henry Ford had rebuilt for the 1929 celebration of the fiftieth anniversary of the lightbulb, remains open for viewing in Ford's Greenfield Village Museum in Deerfield, Michigan.

MAHATMA GANDHI

"Mahatma" (Great Soul)

October 2, 1869–January 30, 1948

"Why worry one's head over a thing that is inevitable? Why die before one's death?"

~ **GANDHI**'S GRANDNIECES (WEARING GLASSES), WHO WERE WITH HIM WHEN HE WAS SHOT, WATCH OVER HIS BODY AS IT LIES IN STATE AT BIRLA HOUSE.

VITAL STATISTICS

AGE AT DEATH: 78

CAUSE OF DEATH: Gunshot wounds from three bullets fired at point-blank range by an assassin

SURVIVORS: Two grandnieces, Manu and Abha; and three sons, Harilal, Ramdas, and Devadas

CLOSE CALLS: On April 26, 1934, Gandhi was attacked by and barely escaped a mob of his countrymen who opposed his call for equal treatment of the untouchables. Later that year, on June 25, in Poona, India, a bomb was thrown at his car. Another bomb was discovered in Gandhi's garden wall just ten days before his assassination.

LAST WORDS: "He Ram." ("Oh, God.")

HIS LIFE

The son of a minister to a maharaja, Mohandas Karamchand Gandhi was raised in a middle-class household in Porbandar, India, and was born to the caste of grocers from which his surname is derived. Following Hindu practice, Gandhi was betrothed before the age of seven, but his fiancé died prematurely. A second betrothal ended the same way. His parents then arranged a third engagement, which resulted in marriage six years later when Gandhi was thirteen. That marriage lasted sixty years.

As a young man, Gandhi studied law in England and worked as an attorney in Bombay before moving to South Africa, where discrimination against Indian settlers was widespread and humiliating. He spent twenty years working against injustices there and, after numerous imprisonments and beatings, developed and first practiced nonviolent civil disobedience.

Upon returning to India in 1915, Gandhi became involved in the nationalist movement to free India from British colonial rule, most notably after the 1919 massacre at Amritsar, where hundreds of his unarmed countrymen were gunned down by British soldiers. Gandhi developed his passive resistance movement, known as *satyagraha* (holding to the truth), in 1920 and became a major figure in the Indian National Congress.

He opposed foreign domination of his homeland and advocated peaceful noncooperation with Great Britain, leading boycotts of British goods, especially imported cloth, and protesting unfair taxes. He abandoned Western clothing and customs in favor of homespun garments, and he spun cotton and led prayer vigils to underscore the importance of manual labor and spiritual well being. Gandhi was jailed many times for his beliefs, but this only increased his popularity and influence. He organized rallies and marches and resorted to hunger strikes that overwhelmingly turned the tide of world sentiment against the British.

Gandhi rallied his countrymen to accompany him on a 240-mile march to the sea in 1930 denouncing the oppressive British Salt Tax, a protest for which he was imprisoned. Released so that he could participate in the Indian Round-Table Conference in London in 1931, he lived among the poor while in England, and when he returned home he began a fast to demand rights for the lowest caste of Indian society, the untouchables, an unpopular position in both Britain and India. He was later jailed again as a political prisoner without privileges.

Between 1935 and 1945, the British reluctantly offered the Indian people various forms of tethered independence, which were rejected by Gandhi and his successor in the Congress Party, Jawaharlal Nehru, because they fell short of offering total independence.

In May 1942, Gandhi finally demanded that the British leave India. He promised complete support of Britain's war effort against the Japanese in exchange for immediate independence; Britain said no. Mounting a party-sanctioned nonviolent rebellion in August of that year, Gandhi was again imprisoned, at age seventy-three, conducting several "fasts until death" while behind bars. He was released once during his twenty-one-month incarceration, so that he could witness the cremation of his wife, who died in February 1944. In May of that year, Gandhi was released due to poor health, and, once free, he resumed the fight for Indian sovereignty.

Three years later, England finally sanctioned India's independence, but only after partitioning the Muslim and Hindu populations into the separate states of India and Pakistan. Gandhi was bitterly disappointed at the compromise and was absent from Independence Day ceremonies on August 14, 1947. Gandhi continued to employ nonviolent tactics. Just two weeks before his death, he began another fast to call for harmony in Delhi between the competing religious faiths there—Hindu, Muslim, and Sikh. After five days, the communities agreed to live peacefully.

On Friday, January 30, 1948, walking arm in arm with his grandnieces through the garden at Birla house, his residence, en route to the place where he conducted daily prayer services, Gandhi was approached by a Hindu extremist, who shot him three times; the assassin was a fanatic who mistakenly assumed that Gandhi had supported the partition between India and Pakistan. It was evident to all that Gandhi's wounds were mortal, so his bullet-ridden body was immediately transported to his spartan room. Twenty-five minutes later Gandhi was dead.

BEST KNOWN FOR:	His simple way of living; his practice of non-violence
FIRST JOB:	Lawyer
AVOCATION:	Spinning cotton

RITES OF PASSAGE

While Gandhi's practices of fasting, vegetarianism, prayer, and opposition to industrialization were not always understood outside of India, his benevolence was globally felt. When he was murdered only a year after India achieved independence, the world was stunned.

THE FUNERAL

After the initial shock of his death, his grandnieces and two of his sons, Ramdas and Devadas, said prayers and quickly performed the ritual Hindu preparations for cremation. Three of India's most celebrated figures came to mourn at Gandhi's bedside: Prime Minister Jawaharlal Nehru; Vallabhbhai Patel, leader of Gandhi's Congress Party and the Home Minister of India; and India's last British representative and Gandhi's supporter, Governor General Louis Mountbatten, who scattered rose petals over his friend's body.

RITUAL FOR THE DEAD According to Gandhi's wishes and orthodox Hindu custom, he was to be cremated within twenty-four hours of his death. For this ceremony, his grandnieces, Manu and Abha, wrapped his freshly bathed body in a simple homespun sheet of his own making and placed it upon a wooden plank surrounded by rose and jasmine petals. They spelled out the words *He Rama* (Oh, God) on his forehead in laurel leaves and *Om* (God) at his feet in rose petals and anointed his chest with sandalwood and saffron paste. His family and friends gathered to sing hymns and recite prayers; in place of the traditional garlands of marigolds draped at the deceased's neck, the family lovingly placed a coil of Gandhi's own spun cotton that he had completed that very day.

By the time the news of Gandhi's death was confirmed, the crowds surrounding the house had swelled to the thousands, and it became clear that the family could not accommodate all who wanted to pay their respects in person. The family placed the martyred Mahatma in full view on a second-floor balcony, where he rested throughout the night on a simple cot illuminated by five oil lamps representing air, earth, fire, water, and unifying light.

THE CREMATION CEREMONY Governor General Louis Mountbatten offered his own bodyguard troops and armored vehicles to transport the deceased through the throngs to the cremation grounds. As ironic as it was for the military of India's former colonizer to orchestrate the funeral procession for Gandhi, Patel and Nehru deemed it a necessary precaution. In Bombay, rioting had already claimed fifteen lives and no one wanted hysteria or upheaval to mar this tribute to the most nonviolent of public figures. Consequently, the military and the British ensured the final delivery of this peaceful nationalist to his funeral pyre.

On the morning of January 31, the cortege left Birla house for Raj Ghat, the cremation grounds on the banks of the Jumma River. It would take nearly six hours to travel the five miles through the streets of Old and New Delhi. Although there was relative order in the streets, the outpouring of grief was unrestrained and monumental. Over a million people lined the cortege route, and another million witnessed the funeral fire. For one day the barriers of history, culture, and religion dissolved into a mass of tears and regret—Hindus wept next to Muslims, Brahmins next to untouchables, women next to men, Indians next to foreigners. The man who had freed India from its colonial shackles was free at last from his corporeal bonds.

Gandhi's small body rested among rose, marigold, and jasmine petals thrown onto the bier by his devotees. Upon arrival at the Jumma River, the wooden plank holding the Indian leader was passed overhead by the crowd before finally reaching its destination. Set high on top of a pyre of sandalwood logs, Gandhi's head pointed to the north, in keeping with Hindu custom.

According to Hindu practice, Gandhi's firstborn son, Harilal, should have led his father's orthodox Hindu funeral services, but at the time of Gandhi's death, Harilal, a destitute alcoholic, was estranged from his father. Therefore Gandhi's second son, Ramdas, circled the pyre five times before setting it alight, while Hindu monks chanted mantras nearby. The police could barely contain the wailing crowds as several women tried to throw themselves onto Gandhi's fiery bier in the Hindu tradition of *suttee,* in which the widow follows her husband to the afterworld. As the flames grew into walls of fire, the crowd cried out, *"Mahatma Gandhi amar ho gaye"* (Mahatma Gandhi has become immortal).

The devoted people remained throughout the night and into the next morning while the embers cooled. Nehru left flowers at the base of Gandhi's pyre saying, "Bapuji, here are flowers. Today at least I can offer them to your bones and ashes. Where will I offer them tomorrow and to whom?"

THE DISTRIBUTION OF ASHES Gandhi's ashes were placed in a simple copper urn, and on Thursday, February 12, Gandhi's relatives transported his remains to New Delhi. In harmony with Mahatma's teachings of simplicity, the family traveled in a third-class train compartment.

The train's mobility was difficult despite the efforts of Congress Party volunteers who stood one hundred yards apart along sixty-seven miles of rail, trying to hold back the millions who came to pay homage along the railroad embankments. Upon arrival at Allahabad, the family transferred to a flower-adorned bier set upon an army weapons carrier. The cortege took three hours to cover the five miles to the Ganges River. Accompanied by military troops with their rifles reversed, the procession was showered with rose petals, marigolds, and lotus flowers from low-flying aircraft. At the riverbank, the family climbed aboard an amphibious army vehicle, painted white, which traveled to the middle of the Ganges River for the final ceremony. Witnessing Gandhi's final farewell from the shore were 3 million of his bereaved followers.

Hindu belief maintains that the soul is released from worldly wanderings twelve days after cremation. This would be Gandhi's moment of spiritual freedom. With the river-stage set, the sounds of flutes, Vedic chanting, bells ringing, and people praying wafted over the water. Thousands of mourners covered in holy sandalwood paste waded into the Ganges, throwing symbols of their devotion—flowers, sweets, even hair—into the waters. Devotees swallowed three ceremonial mouthfuls of the river water as Gandhi's ritual farewell began.

Ramdas, who had lit the funeral pyre, now took his father's ashes and mixed them in the urn with milk from a sacred cow. After chanting a final hymn with his family and Gandhi's close friends, including Nehru and Patel, Ramdas poured the contents of the urn into the river. Each mourner on the floating army vehicle tossed rose petals on the spot where Gandhi's mortal remains had united with the water. The current rapidly swept them out of sight.

Two weeks later, the last British troops left India.

NEWS OF THE DAY
JANUARY 31, 1948

GANDHI IS KILLED BY A HINDU

INDIA SHAKEN, WORLD MOURNS; 15 DIE IN RIOTING IN BOMBAY

ALL BRITAIN HONORS GANDHI; TRUMAN DEPLORES TRAGEDY

ORVILLE WRIGHT, 76, IS DEAD IN DAYTON

ARMY GETS ATOMIC ENERGY PRIORITY

AROUND THE WORLD

At the United Nations in New York, a memorial service was held in the council meeting room, with eulogies delivered by both the Pakistani and Indian representatives. The UN flag was ordered to fly at half-staff for three days in New York and Geneva, during which time none of the fifty-seven member flags was raised.

In England, King George VI, members of Parliament, and every political party, including the Communists, offered tributes to the man who had resisted British colonial rule for more than forty years. Prime Minister Atlee said he hoped that the Indian leader's spirit "will continue to animate his fellow countrymen and will plead for peace and concord."

BEYOND THE GRAVE

Gandhi was the highest paid recording artist of his time. The British Press reported that Gandhi earned $200,000 for making one phonographic record in 1932, *The Justification of God.*

When Gandhi traveled to Britain to attend the 1931 Indian Round-Table Conference in London he met royalty and heads of state alike while wearing his homespun cloth shawl and loincloth. On his return voyage, he stopped in Rome and met with Premier Mussolini, but he was denied a meeting with the pope because of his "revealing" costume.

ODD COINCIDENCES

Lord Mountbatten would be assassinated thirty-one years later by an Irish Republic Army terrorist using a bomb planted on his fishing boat in north-west Ireland.

❧ THE GREAT PACIFIST'S FUNERAL PYRE BURNS ON THE
BANK OF THE JUMMA RIVER IN NEW DEHLI.

JIM HENSON

"Jim"

September 24, 1936–May 16, 1990

"Puppetry is a good way of hiding."

≈ **HENSON**, WITH FRIENDS

VITAL STATISTICS

AGE AT DEATH: 53

CAUSE OF DEATH: Cardiac arrest following aggressive streptococcus pneumonia

SURVIVORS: His estranged wife, Jane Anne Nebel; five children: Lisa Marie, Cheryl Lee, Brian David, John Paul, and Heather Beth; and his father, Paul Ransom Henson

HIS LIFE

Born in Greenville, Mississippi, but raised in a Maryland suburb of Washington, D.C., the shy young Henson became enthralled by the new medium of television. Upon graduation from high school, Henson and a friend auditioned as puppeteers for a children's show on a local television station. They secured that spot but it only lasted a few weeks. As a freshman at the University of Maryland studying theater arts, Henson landed another puppet show at a rival television station. *Sam and Friends,* a five-minute program, ran twice a day for six years and introduced Henson to the challenges of live television, the demands of which kept him and his future wife, fellow puppeteer Jane Nebel, working constantly. A lanky, thoughtful man, Henson never intended to pursue puppetry as a career but saw it as a means to produce television shows. His early success as a student, earning $5 a show and then $100 a week for *Sam and Friends,* helped redirect him.

In 1958, Henson traveled to Europe and studied the art of using marionettes and hand puppets—the word *Muppet,* which he used to refer to his creations, is a combination of the words *marionette* and *puppet.* Later that year, Henson snagged the first of his eighteen Emmy Awards for excellence in television programming.

Henson also created popular television commercials featuring his Muppets, spots that helped pay the bills, but he had bigger dreams for his foam-and-felt creatures: a full-length television show. He continued to build a larger audience by making frequent guest appearances on *The Tonight Show* with Steve Allen, *The Ed Sullivan Show,* and *The Jimmy Dean Show,* and he and his Muppets were quickly becoming stars.

Henson and his alter ego, Kermit the Frog, delighted audiences with their wry humor, innocence, and quirky optimism. Colleagues noted that mild-mannered, workaholic Henson was not nearly as witty without a sock on his hand. His persistence paid off when, in 1969, Henson collaborated with the Children's Television Workshop to produce the award-winning children's television show *Sesame Street.* On the show, Henson's Muppet creatures—Big Bird, Bert and Ernie, Grover, Cookie Monster, and a host of others—taught preschoolers how to count, write, and enjoy learning. The characters were lovable yet flawed; witty yet silly; moral yet lighthearted; mischievous yet kind; they appealed to children and adults alike.

Banking on the global appeal of Kermit and the *Sesame Street* crew, Jim Henson hoped to produce his own show on commercial television. A British producer took the plunge with Henson in 1976, funding *The Muppet Show.* That show, hosted by Kermit and introducing the porcine starlet Miss Piggy, became an instant success, pairing live performers with the lovable Muppets. On air until 1981, *The Muppet Show,* which was first broadcast in Great Britain before airing in the United States, was seen weekly by more than 250 million viewers worldwide. After its five-year run, *The Muppet Show* went into immediate syndication in more than 106 countries. The show's continued popularity spawned millions of dollars' worth of licensing products and a series of successful feature films starring Jim Henson's beloved menagerie.

Henson went on to produce two non-Muppet movies, *The Dark Crystal* (1982) and *Labyrinth* (1986), experimenting with computer technology and animatronics to manipulate his fantastic creatures, and he created the Yoda character for George Lucas's space fantasy, *The Empire Strikes Back* (1980). Henson returned to television to create the children's television show *Fraggle Rock* in 1983 and the animated series *Muppet Babies* in 1984, all the while continuing to produce the Muppets segments on *Sesame Street*.

Henson fell ill with a sore throat and a cough after taping a television appearance in California in early May 1990, but proceeded to keep to his grueling schedule as his cold worsened. He did little but seek bed rest, thinking he would improve on his own. Finally, at the urging of his estranged wife, Jane, he agreed to go to New York Hospital in the early hours of May 16. Unable to breathe by the time he arrived, doctors reported that his vital organs were already shutting down as a result of pneumonia. His wife, children, and many of his lifelong associates waited in a grim vigil. Twenty hours later, after suffering two cardiac arrests, Jim Henson died.

Had Henson gone for treatment eight hours sooner, the virulent strain of pneumonia that killed him could still have been contained.

BEST KNOWN FOR:	Kermit the Frog
FIRST JOB:	Puppeteer
AVOCATIONS:	Collecting expensive cars and antiques

RITES OF PASSAGE

Four years before his death, while on vacation in the south of Europe with a friend and in a pensive mood, Henson wrote letters to each of his children, to be opened after his death. In one, he made his wishes for his funeral known.

THE FUNERAL

At noon on Monday, May 21, the funeral service commenced at the Cathedral of St. John the Divine in New York City, accommodating nearly five thousand guests. In keeping with Henson's wishes, the ceremony was a jubilant one. Henson had requested "a nice, friendly little service" and "a rousing Dixieland band." He also stipulated that no one should wear black. His family obliged, calling the colorful service a "celebration of life."

THE SERVICE Upon entering the cathedral, mourners received colorful foam butterflies dangling on wands along with their programs, which featured a wish from Henson: "Please watch out for each other and love and forgive everybody. It's a good life. Enjoy it." While friends and family filed into the church, an organist played an improvised version of the *Sesame Street* theme song, "Sunny Day."

The services began with the Dirty Dozen Brass Band playing a dirge while marching up the central aisle ahead of the clergy, choir, and family. Singer Harry Belafonte paid tribute to his friend, acknowledging, "There is no question about Jim Henson's great artistry and the extent to which we have all been touched by it. But greater than his artistry was his humanity." Belafonte sang his own composition, "Turn the World Around," backed by three singers, while the congregation waved their butterfly wands. Belafonte was followed by an audio recording of Jim Henson as Kermit the Frog singing "Rainbow Connection."

A tribute by *Sesame Street*'s most identifiable Muppet, Big Bird, was a showstopper. Alone at the altar, the costumed actor Carroll Spinney sang Kermit's signature song, "It's Not Easy Being Green." At the conclusion, the seven-foot-tall yellow bird bowed and said, "Thank you, Kermit."

Jane Henson introduced her five children, and Brian, the eldest son, read portions of the letters that his father had left each of them, including the following: "Don't feel bad that I've gone. I look forward to seeing all of you when you come over . . . This may all seem silly to you guys, but what the hell, I'm gone and who can argue with me?"

Next, a band of Henson puppeteers, performing in street clothes with Muppets on their hands, sang a Muppets medley using character voices, their sorrow visible on human, as well as Muppet, faces. Finally, the Dirty Dozen Brass Band closed the service by performing the one song Henson had requested, "When the Saints Go Marching In."

FINAL RESTING PLACE Jim Henson was cremated. The whereabouts of his ashes are unknown.

NEWS OF THE DAY
MAY 17, 1990

SOUTH AFRICA TO ADMIT ALL RACES AS PATIENTS IN ITS PUBLIC HOSPITALS

SAMMY DAVIS JR. DIES AT 64; TOP SHOWMAN BROKE BARRIERS

JIM HENSON, PUPPETEER, DIES; THE MUPPETS' CREATOR WAS 53

AROUND THE WORLD
On July 2, 1990, at St. Paul's Cathedral in London, more than two thousand friends and associates gathered to pay respects. The hallowed cathedral, where Princess Diana and Prince Charles had been married and Sir Winston Churchill's funeral service was held, was invaded by Muppets with farewell tributes.

BEYOND THE GRAVE
LAST WISHES
Before he died, Jim Henson had been negotiating with the Walt Disney Company to sell his company; in August 1989 Disney officials announced their intent to acquire Henson Associates. The sale, estimated to be worth more than $100 million, would have been Henson's legacy to his children. He had been scheduled to continue negotiations with Disney the week he died. The deal unraveled over Disney's desire to own licensing rights to Kermit and the *Sesame Street* characters, which Henson had not wanted to relinquish.

MEMORIALS AND TRIBUTES
On November 21, 1990, a special Thanksgiving production, "The Muppets Celebrate Jim Henson," was aired on CBS. The hour-long presentation showed clips from Henson's twenty years of television puppetry.

In 2000, The Jim Henson Company moved its headquarters to the Los Angeles studio location once owned by Charlie Chaplin. On June 23, 2000, the company unveiled a twelve-foot statue of Kermit the Frog dressed as Chaplin's Little Tramp. The memorial to the two visionaries greets visitors entering the studio compound.

THE HEREAFTER
Henson's children inherited his company and the rights to the Muppets. They decided to keep alive the characters to which their father had given voice—notably Kermit, Ernie, and Rowlf. Kermit did not appear for six months after his creator's death, but the family felt that the devoted Muppets' audience would sustain a much greater loss if Kermit disappeared entirely.

BIG BIRD SINGS KERMIT THE FROG'S (AND **HENSON**'S) SIGNATURE SONG, "IT'S NOT EASY BEING GREEN," AT HENSON'S MEMORIAL SERVICE AT THE CATHEDRAL OF ST. JOHN THE DIVINE IN NEW YORK CITY.

GRACE KELLY

"Princess Grace"

November 12, 1929–September 14, 1982

"I would like to be remembered as trying to do my job well, being understanding and kind."

IN DEATH, THE PRINCESS CLUTCHES A ROSARY IN HER WHITE SATIN COFFIN.

VITAL STATISTICS

AGE AT DEATH: 52

CAUSE OF DEATH: Cerebral hemorrhage sustained in an auto accident when her car plummeted off the cliffs of Monaco

SURVIVORS: Her husband, Prince Rainier III of Monaco; three children, Princess Caroline, Prince Albert, and Princess Stephanie; two sisters; a brother; and her eighty-three-year-old mother

HER LIFE

Even in infancy, Grace Kelly was stunningly beautiful. The third of four children of a prominent Irish family in Philadelphia, she moved to New York after high school to pursue modeling and acting. In 1949, she graduated from the American Academy of Dramatic Arts, where her cool demeanor and smoldering beauty had caught the attention of Hollywood directors.

After making her film debut in 1951, Kelly performed in an ingenue role opposite Gary Cooper in the 1952 Western *High Noon.* She starred in ten more films, sharing the screen with some of Hollywood's most dashing leading men, including Cary Grant, Bing Crosby, Frank Sinatra, Clark Gable, and William Holden. In 1954, she won an Academy Award for her performance opposite Bing Crosby in *The Country Girl.*

A year later the twenty-five-year-old beauty met Prince Rainier of Monaco's Grimaldi dynasty while filming Alfred Hitchcock's *To Catch a Thief* in Monte Carlo. During their second meeting, which occurred in the United States, the couple fell in love. Four days later, with her parents' consent, they decided to wed.

Their Roman Catholic wedding at the Cathedral of St. Nicholas in tiny Monaco received unprecedented media coverage. Eleven hundred guests attended, and sixteen hundred journalists mobbed the Riviera city for two days of celebration on April 18 and 19, 1956.

In her twenty-six years as Her Serene Highness, Princess Grace devoted much of her time to her family and to charitable works, winning the hearts of the Monegasques. Monaco had been best known as a tax haven and the home of the Monte Carlo Casino, but under Princess Grace's watchful eye it evolved into an elegant and caring commonwealth. She brought a concern for Monaco's people and culture to the four hundred and sixty-seven-acre oasis by renovating and expanding the Monaco hospital, promoting breast-feeding, and raising money for other causes.

On Monday, September 13, 1982, Princess Grace and her youngest child, Princess Stephanie, then only seventeen years old, were returning by car from France to Monaco. On the winding turns of the cliff-hanging roadways overlooking the Côte d'Azur, the car hurtled down a forty-five-foot cliff and burst into flames. Princess Stephanie escaped with severe bruising and shock, but Princess Grace sustained multiple fractures to her collarbone, thighbone, and ribs and she never regained consciousness. Firefighters transported the monarch to Princess Grace Polyclinic, the hospital she had rebuilt, where brain scans indicated that she had also suffered a massive stroke. She died the following day after Prince Rainier, in consensus with his two elder children, agreed to remove her life support.

BEST KNOWN FOR: Her fairy-tale marriage

FIRST JOB: Fashion model

AVOCATION: Flower arrangement

RITES OF PASSAGE

THE PREPARATION

After her death, Princess Grace's body was taken from the hospital to the Palatine Chapel in the west wing of the Grimaldi family's residential palace.

PAYING RESPECTS

On Wednesday, September 15, the Monte Carlo public paid respects at the Palatine Chapel. There, in an open, silk-lined casket, Her Serene Highness lay dressed in a white gown, adorned by her wedding ring and clutching a rosary. Her bier was illuminated by four white candles and surrounded by four white-uniformed palace guards who stood at attention while the tearful Monegasques waited in line to bid the princess good-bye.

THE FUNERAL

THE PROCESSION At 10:30 A.M. on Saturday, September 18, a bugle flourish heralded the commencement of Princess Grace's funeral. Accompanied by Princess Caroline and Prince Albert, Prince Rainier III followed a priest who led the funeral cortege out of the black-velvet-draped palace entrance into the streets of Monte Carlo. Princess Stephanie, still in the hospital, was unable to attend. The public lined the avenues in silent tribute.

The cortege consisted of Monaco's white-uniformed, red-plumed carabineers and twenty pallbearers in white robes who carried the Princess's white-draped coffin one-third of a mile to the Cathedral of St. Nicholas.

THE SERVICE Once inside, the coffin lay behind the altar of the Chapel of Princes underneath black crepe drapery. During the requiem mass, the Archbishop of Monaco delivered his homily, entitled "We are united in pain." Prince Rainier wept openly in the chapel where he had exchanged marriage vows a quarter of a century earlier.

Eight hundred mourners filled the cathedral, including Irish president Patrick Hillery; actor Cary Grant; Barbara Sinatra, wife of the princess's *High Society* costar Frank Sinatra; Prince Bertil of Sweden; Princess Benedikta of Denmark; Grand Duchess Josephine of Luxembourg; and race-car champion Jackie Stewart. Nancy Reagan, Danielle Mitterand, and Princess Diana sat together.

Musical selections included Samuel Barber's *Adagio for Strings,* selections from Bach, and part of Haydn's Fourth Symphony. The Gospel reading was from the Book of John ("In my Father's house are many mansions . . .").

FINAL RESTING PLACE Grace Kelly was buried in the Grimaldi crypt, under the cathedral where her funeral mass had been conducted. Although the Prince had intended for the burial to follow the mass, he postponed the entombment until the following week. A second funeral mass for the public, which was also attended by the Grimaldi family, ran overtime, taxing the exhausted and bereft Prince Rainier.

NEWS OF THE DAY

SEPTEMBER 15, 1982

PRINCESS GRACE IS DEAD AFTER RIVIERA CAR CRASH

GEMAYEL OF LEBANON IS KILLED
IN BOMB BLAST AT PARTY OFFICES

AROUND THE WORLD

In her hometown of Philadelphia, Princess Grace had been treated like royalty long before her marriage to Rainier. When she died, the City of Brotherly Love mounted its own tribute on Friday, September 17, 1982. City flags flew at half-staff, and in the Cathedral of Saints Peter and Paul, John Cardinal Krol said mass before fifteen hundred congregates including forty

∿ THE PRINCESS AND CARY GRANT, OVERLOOKING MONTE CARLO FROM THE CLIFFS ABOVE, IN A SCENE FROM ALFRED HITCHCOCK'S *TO CATCH A THIEF*.

family members, former Philadelphia mayor Frank Rizzo, and Mayor William J. Green. The preceding day, the family's local church, St. Bridget's Church in East Falls, held a memorial mass for the princess for one hundred and fifty mourners, many from her old neighborhood.

BEYOND THE GRAVE

During the royal couple's two-day marriage celebration in 1956, the police arrested two pickpockets who had successfully infiltrated the reception by posing as priests.

ODD COINCIDENCES

The site of Princess Diana's death in Paris, fifteen years later, would bear an eerie resemblance to that of Princess Grace's death. In addition to sending thousands of condolence letters, the public memorialized the site of Grace Kelly's car crash on the twisting roadway known as the "middle corniche," near Cap-d'Ail, leaving floral bouquets for months after her burial. A similar shrine to Princess Diana sprang up on the right bank of the Seine after she, too, perished in a violent automobile accident. Neither princess had been wearing a safety belt.

MYSTERIOUS CIRCUMSTANCES

The police were never able to determine, and Princess Stephanie has not recalled, why the car went of control, who was driving, or whether Princess Grace suffered a stroke before or after the crash. Rumors have clouded the issue, contributing to an oft-repeated conjecture that the two occupants were arguing, causing Princess Grace to suffer a stroke and lose control of the Rover 3500. Testimony from the first person on the scene after the crash indicated that Princess Stephanie was pinned on the left side of the vehicle and was removed through the window. It has never been disclosed whether the steering wheel was on the right or left side of the British-made car.

LAST WISHES

Princess Grace had dreamed of building a home on her family's ancestral property in Ireland. Rainier completed her project posthumously.

JOHN F. KENNEDY

"Jack"

May 29, 1917–November 22, 1963

"Ask not what your country can do for you—ask what you can do for your country."

KENNEDY, WITH HIS WIFE JACKIE,
IN A DALLAS MOTORCADE, NOVEMBER 22ND, 1963,
MOMENTS BEFORE HE WAS ASSASSINATED.

VITAL STATISTICS

AGE AT DEATH: 46

CAUSE OF DEATH: Gunshot wound to the head from an assassin's bullet

SURVIVORS: His wife, Jacqueline Bouvier Kennedy; a daughter, Caroline; a son, John Jr.; two brothers, Robert and Edward; three sisters, Jean Smith, Patricia Lawford, and Eunice Shriver; and his parents, Rose and Joseph Kennedy

CLOSE CALLS: At the age of thirty-seven, Kennedy nearly died during the first of a series of spinal operations. A Roman Catholic priest administered last rites, the first of four times he would receive the sacrament.

HIS LIFE

Born of Irish immigrants and raised in Massachusetts, Jack Kennedy was the second son of nine children. Early in the century, his father, Joseph, had emerged as a powerful force in politics, using his influence to amass a personal fortune. His wife, Rose, was the well-connected daughter of Boston mayor John "Honey Fitz" Fitzgerald. Together they forged a dynasty of Kennedys, in whom they instilled great ambitions.

Jack Kennedy attended the prestigious preparatory school Choate and, after a brief enrollment at Princeton, graduated from Harvard University in 1940. While at Harvard he wrote a thesis on England's unpreparedness for World War II, which became a best-selling book, *Why England Slept.* Headed for graduate school at Stanford University in 1941, he changed directions and accepted a commission as lieutenant in the U.S. Navy, where in 1943 his

rescue of crewmen from his PT boat while under attack in the Pacific earned him two medals and a hero's status.

Athletic good looks and an easygoing manner made Kennedy's transition from war hero to political candidate an easy one. In 1946, with the financial support of his father, Kennedy secured a seat in the U.S. Congress representing Boston's eleventh district, and he was reelected to the House of Representatives in 1948 and 1950.

In 1952, by an unexpectedly large margin, Jack Kennedy defeated incumbent Republican Henry Cabot Lodge for a seat in the U.S. Senate representing Massachusetts. In September 1953, at age thirty-six, he married Jacqueline Bouvier, twelve years his junior, at a celebrated high-society wedding. Back injuries kept him out of some of the Senate's most controversial anti-Communist debates, but the senator used his convalescence to write *Profiles in Courage,* which later received the 1957 Pulitzer Prize.

After nearly earning the vice-presidential nomination on Democrat Adlai Stevenson's ticket in 1956, Kennedy went to bat for Stevenson, stumping on the campaign trail in twenty-eight states and learning the ins and outs of presidential politics up close. In 1958, he was elected for a second U.S. Senate term in the largest landslide in Massachusetts's history and took aim at the White House.

At the 1960 Democratic Convention in Los Angeles, Kennedy won the nomination for president on the first ballot, adding Senator Lyndon B. Johnson from Texas as his running mate. The forty-three-year-old Kennedy's formidable Republican challenger was Vice President Richard M. Nixon, who had benefited from his eight years as Eisenhower's second-in-command while the country was experiencing economic prosperity and peace. The nature of the 1960 presidential campaign changed U.S. politics for the remainder of the century, with the two candidates squaring off in four televised debates and heavily employing broadcast advertising.

Kennedy won on November 8, 1960, by a narrow popular vote and a more comfortable electoral vote, the youngest man ever elected as president. His second child, John Fitzgerald Kennedy Jr., was born less than three weeks later, on Thanksgiving Day.

President Kennedy's 1,037 days in office had stellar highs and dangerous lows. The young, glamorous couple represented hope and prosperity and the Kennedys' inner circle was later dubbed "Camelot" after the legend of King Arthur's court. An upbeat nation celebrated space exploration as Alan Shepard became the first American in space in May 1961, followed by John Glenn's orbit of the earth a year later. In addition, with the founding of the Peace Corps, Kennedy spearheaded America's global humanitarian effort. Yet the young president blundered badly in 1961 when he approved an invasion of Cuba, to be backed by the Central Intelligence Agency (CIA). Known as the "Bay of Pigs" invasion, its mission was to incite anti-Castro rebels to call on the United States to overthrow Fidel Castro's regime. The mission backfired and Kennedy admitted the covert U.S. role in the operation, tarnishing his prestige at home and abroad.

On the heels of the Bay of Pigs, Kennedy met his greatest challenge, the rise of the Cold War. The Soviets, led by Premier Nikita Khrushchev, erected the Berlin Wall, tested more powerful and destructive nuclear weapons, and began to build missiles in Cuba in October 1962, setting off the Cuban Missile Crisis. Erecting a naval blockade of Cuba, the United States prohibited Soviet ships from delivering military components. After nearly two weeks in a standoff, Khrushchev offered a compromise wherein the Soviets would dismantle their Cuban missile sites in exchange for a U.S. promise not to invade the tiny island. Kennedy accepted Khrushchev's proposal and later agreed to remove American missiles aimed at the Soviet Union that were based in Turkey. The world sighed in relief and Kennedy's popularity soared.

The last year of Kennedy's administration saw more focus on economic development, foreign aid, and civil rights issues. His administration's commitment to end desegregation helped pave the way for Dr. Martin Luther King Jr. and other civil rights activists to reach a national audience, culminating in August 1963 in the March on Washington.

The legacy that Kennedy left in foreign affairs was double-edged. Responsible for creating the popular Peace Corps, Kennedy also supported the corrupt regime of President Ngo Dinh Diem of South Vietnam. His support of the South Vietnamese government embroiled the nation in one of the costliest and most controversial military incursions in its history.

On Friday, November 22, 1963, President Kennedy and his wife made a visit to Texas. After a morning speech in Fort Worth, the couple flew to neighboring Dallas and were met by Governor John Connally and his wife, Nellie. Along the short motorcade route through downtown Dallas, a sniper, Lee Harvey Oswald, shot the president and the governor at 12:30 P.M.

Three shots were fired. The first hit Kennedy in the back, causing only minor injury. The second hit Connally. The third shattered the back of Kennedy's head and he died almost instantly. An amateur movie, known as the "Zapruder" film, recorded the terrible scene. The president was rushed to Parkland Memorial Hospital, where he was pronounced dead at 1:00 P.M. central time. Vice President Lyndon Johnson was sworn in on board Air Force One as the thirty-sixth president of the United States ninety-nine minutes later.

BEST KNOWN FOR: His youth, vigor, and charisma

FIRST JOB: Naval lieutenant; reporter for Hearst's International News Service

AVOCATION: Writing

RITES OF PASSAGE

The president's body was immediately returned in a bronze casket to Air Force One at Love Airfield in Dallas, where Mrs. Kennedy looked on as Vice President Johnson took the oath of office. They departed for Andrews Air Force Base, outside of Washington, D.C., arriving before six o'clock.

THE PREPARATION

Attorney General Robert F. Kennedy, brother of the slain president, met Air Force One and accompanied Mrs. Kennedy and the flag-draped coffin in a hearse to Bethesda Naval Hospital. There, doctors performed an autopsy while his widow and family waited nearby in the V.I.P. suite throughout the night.

When the autopsy and embalming had been completed, Mrs. Kennedy and Robert Kennedy returned to the White House at half past four in the morning of Saturday, November 23. Mrs. Kennedy, still wearing her blood-stained skirt, had not rested for nearly twenty-four hours.

Mrs. Kennedy did not want an open-casket funeral, but members of the cabinet felt it would be unavoidable. The idea was abandoned after Robert Kennedy and eight of his brother's most trusted advisers peered into the coffin and decided against it.

PAYING RESPECTS

The president's flag-draped coffin was placed in the East Room of the White House. An honor guard composed of servicemen from all branches of the military stood on duty while two priests representing Catholic and Protestant faiths remained in prayer.

At ten o'clock that morning Mrs. Kennedy, Caroline, and John Jr. entered the East Room, knelt at the coffin under a black-draped chandelier, and prayed. Father John Cavanaugh, a family friend and former president of Notre Dame University, conducted a mass at 10:30 for seventy-five family members and friends.

After the mass, elected officials and associates came to the White House to pay respects, including John W. McCormack, Speaker of the House; President and Mrs. Johnson; former presidents Dwight D. Eisenhower and Harry Truman; cabinet members; and senior staff of the late president.

On the day of the assassination, most businesses, schools, and offices closed early, and people gathered in places of worship, or with loved ones at home, seeking consolation. Theaters, movie houses, and nightclubs canceled performances. Times Square was deserted and the normally brilliant hub of New York activity was darkened as advertisers one by one shut down their bright marquee-sized signs. Huddled around television sets, Americans watched as the funeral activities, and the police manhunt for the assassin, unfolded.

At 10:00 A.M. on Saturday, November 23, more than twenty-five hundred people crowded into St. Patrick's Cathedral in Manhattan for a pontifical requiem mass; a flag-covered catafalque represented the slain president's coffin. The service concluded with the singing of the national anthem as the

THE SLAIN PRESIDENT'S COFFIN IS LED TO THE CAPITOL BUILDING.

congregation and clergy were awash in tears. Pope Paul VI granted special permission to American Catholic churches to hold requiem masses for their slain president on Sunday, November 24, since requiem masses are ordinarily prohibited on Sundays. St. Patrick's held a morning service on Sunday and two services on Monday, one specifically for the United Nations delegation in New York.

Also on Saturday, people began arriving in the nation's capital in anticipation of the president's lying in state. By early Sunday morning crowds had gathered across from the White House and filled the East Plaza in front of the Capitol building.

The first official funeral procession—to place President Kennedy's body in state in the Capitol Rotunda—began on Sunday, November 24, shortly before one o'clock. Drawn by six gray horses, a caisson, the same artillery carriage that had borne the coffin of President Franklin D. Roosevelt in 1945, pulled up to the black-draped north portico of the White House. Eight enlisted men from all the branches of the armed services served as body bearers and laid the president's coffin on the caisson. It slowly made its way from the White House down Pennsylvania Avenue to the Capitol building.

A police escort, five military drummers, a company of Navy enlisted men, and military advisers to President Kennedy, led by General Maxwell Taylor, walked at a funeral pace (one hundred paces per minute) ahead of the caisson. Immediately behind the carriage came a riderless horse, Sardar, a thoroughbred owned by Mrs. Kennedy. The gelding bore a saddle with boots worn in reverse, the symbol of a fallen leader.

A lead-paneled limousine carrying Mrs. Kennedy, her children, the Attorney General, and President and Mrs. Johnson followed immediately, with ten more cars bearing family members completing the cortege. Security was heavy along the route, with bayonet-equipped soldiers standing at parade rest every twenty-five feet. Three hundred thousand people lined the wide avenues, twenty deep in many places.

When the cortege arrived at the Capitol fifty minutes later, a twenty-one-gun salute rang out. The body bearers lifted the coffin up the north steps to the Rotunda. Mrs. Kennedy, her children and brother-in-law, and the Johnsons followed. Bathed in sunlight from the Capitol Rotunda's windows, President Kennedy's coffin was placed on the catafalque upon which President Abraham Lincoln had rested ninety-eight years earlier. President Johnson placed a wreath at the head of the coffin. Mrs. Kennedy then knelt before it and prayed. After lightly kissing the coffin, she arose and left the Capitol. Members of the Supreme Court, the Cabinet, and Congress wept. At 2:19 P.M. ABC News finally released the report it had withheld until Mrs. Kennedy was safely in her limousine: the president's assassin, Lee Harvey Oswald, had been murdered even before the cortege had left the White House.

That Sunday afternoon, public viewing began immediately after the dignitaries departed and continued until nine o'clock Monday morning, November 25. By that time, when the bronze doors closed, more than a quarter of a million citizens had paid their final respects, some having waited up to nine hours in thirty-degree weather.

Mrs. Kennedy returned to the Rotunda Monday evening for private prayer. Other evening visitors included Kennedy's mother, Senator Edward Kennedy, and Eunice Kennedy Shriver, all of whom had arrived from the Kennedys' Hyannis Port compound too late to attend the formal ceremony earlier that afternoon. Mrs. Robert Kennedy, Mrs. Edward Kennedy, and the actor Peter Lawford, their brother-in-law, also joined them.

THE FUNERAL

Plans for the funeral had been announced the day after Kennedy's murder. In one of his first acts as president, Lyndon Johnson issued a proclamation designating Monday, November 25, a national day of mourning and asking citizens to "pay their homage of love and reverence to the memory of a great and good man." Governor Rockefeller of New York proclaimed the day a legal holiday in the state, closing banks and stock exchanges. Government offices, schools, and businesses were closed as millions of Americans watched their first presidential funeral on television.

Foreign heads of state and royalty began to arrive in the nation's capital on Sunday. Ninety-two nations were represented by 220 attendees, including England's Prince Philip, a proxy for the pregnant Elizabeth II, Prime Minister Sir Alec Douglas-Home, and British Labor leader Harold Wilson; Emperor Haile Selassie of Ethiopia; President Charles de Gaulle of France; Queen Frederika of Greece; King Baudouin of Belgium; Ludwig Erhard, chancellor of West Germany; Willy Brandt, mayor of Berlin; Eamon De Valera, president of Ireland; U Thant, secretary general of the United Nations; Anastas Mikoyan, first deputy premier of the Soviet Union; and Crown Princess Beatrix of the Netherlands were among the notables. The huge number of diplomats strained American security forces, who would not guarantee their safety.

THE PROCESSION On Monday, November 25, with three television networks covering the proceedings, the caisson slowly repeated its funeral march out of the Capitol Plaza, returning to the White House. Washington's streets were lined with thousands of people standing in the cold autumn air. Military units met the caisson at Constitution Avenue, beginning the official seven-block-long cortege, which included a caparisoned horse, the Marine Corps Band, and distinguished military units from all the services.

Foreign dignitaries had gathered at the White House in anticipation of the walk from the residence to St. Matthew's Cathedral eight blocks away. At 11:35 A.M., as midshipmen were heard singing in the distance, the military procession led the caisson out of the White House gates, and Mrs. Kennedy, flanked by Edward Kennedy and Robert Kennedy, her face covered by a black veil, took her place squarely behind the caisson. The music of the Black Watch bagpipers hung in the air. Behind Mrs. Kennedy walked President Johnson and his wife, followed by the limousine carrying the Kennedy children. World leaders and U.S. officials followed, including the members of the Supreme Court and Cabinet, and former presidents Truman and Eisenhower, who shared a limousine. The only other living president, Herbert Hoover, age eighty-nine, sent his son to represent him.

THE SERVICE Nearly eleven hundred invited guests had gathered at St. Matthew's Cathedral. Two family friends, newsmen Hugh Sidey of *Time* magazine and Ben Bradlee of *Newsweek,* ushered distinguished guests to their pews.

Richard Cardinal Cushing of Boston greeted Mrs. Kennedy at the cathedral's steps and sprinkled holy water on the coffin. When Mrs. Kennedy had been seated, just a few feet from her husband's coffin, Cardinal Cushing began the pontifical requiem mass. Luigi Vena sang Gounod's "Ave Maria" at the request of Mrs. Kennedy, at whose wedding he had also sung the song.

After Communion, the Most Reverend Philip Hannan, the auxiliary bishop of Washington, D.C., delivered an eleven-minute oratory. He reminded the congregates of the president's frequent biblical references, including the following, which Kennedy used in one of his last speeches: "Your old men shall dream dreams, your young men shall see visions, and where there is no vision the people shall perish."

At 1:15 P.M. the clergy followed the crucifix down the central aisle and opened the church doors. Immediately thereafter, the pallbearers carried the coffin out of the church and a military band played "Hail to the Chief." Following the casket, Mrs. Kennedy and her children made their way through the crowded church to the top of the steps.

While John F. Kennedy's coffin was placed for the third and final time atop the caisson, the young John Jr. saluted his father, in what would become one of the most searing images of a generation. It was his third birthday.

The entire Kennedy family stood in silent tribute as the caisson passed, and they then took refuge in their limousines. More than two hundred chauffeured cars awaited the mourners departing St. Matthew's, causing confusion and traffic delays. The funeral cortege slowly departed the church, passed the Lincoln Memorial, and crossed the Memorial Bridge en route to Arlington National Cemetery, with every move of the funeral party being captured by the three television networks.

FINAL RESTING PLACE Despite the confused and chaotic scene at the cathedral, no one missed the Arlington graveside service, a full military burial with honors. The horse-drawn carriage arrived at the cemetery at 2:43 P.M., whereupon fifty jets, representing each of the states in the Union, flew overhead. Air Force One followed, unaccompanied.

Cardinal Cushing delivered graveside prayers, after which military personnel fired the traditional twenty-one-gun salute. An army bugler played "Taps." Next, the body bearers crisply folded the flag covering the slain president's coffin and presented it to his widow. A final three-rifle volley, fired three times in sequence over John Fitzgerald Kennedy's grave, signaled the end of the formal military service. Mrs. Kennedy lit an eternal flame at her hus-

band's grave. Cardinal Cushing and Kennedy's brothers, Bobby and Ted, also lit the flame. The three Kennedys departed, and at 3:34 P.M. the coffin was lowered into the grave.

The official period of national mourning ended thirty days after Kennedy's death, on December 22, when President Johnson honored him in a candle-light service at the Lincoln Memorial in view of his eternal flame on the slope at Arlington National Cemetery across the Potomac River.

NEWS OF THE DAY

NOVEMBER 23, 1963
KENNEDY IS KILLED BY SNIPER AS HE RIDES IN CAR IN DALLAS; JOHNSON SWORN IN ON PLANE

GOV. CONNALLY SHOT; MRS. KENNEDY SAFE

NOVEMBER 24, 1963
KENNEDY'S BODY LIES IN WHITE HOUSE; JOHNSON AT HELM WITH WIDE BACKING; POLICE SAY PRISONER IS THE ASSASSIN

JOHNSON ORDERS DAY OF MOURNING

EVIDENCE AGAINST OSWALD DESCRIBED AS CONCLUSIVE

KHRUSHCHEV PAYS SPECIAL RESPECTS

NOVEMBER 25, 1963
PRESIDENT'S ASSASSIN SHOT TO DEATH IN JAIL CORRIDOR BY A DALLAS CITIZEN; GRIEVING THRONGS VIEW KENNEDY BIER

JOHNSON AFFIRMS AIMS IN VIETNAM

MILLIONS OF VIEWERS SEE OSWALD KILLING ON 2 TV NETWORKS

NOVEMBER 26, 1963

KENNEDY LAID TO REST IN ARLINGTON;
HUSHED NATION WATCHES AND GRIEVES;
WORLD LEADERS PAY TRIBUTE AT GRAVE

OTHER DEATHS
J. D. Tippet of the Dallas police force was shot and killed by Lee Harvey Oswald while apprehending the assassin. He left a wife and three children.

AROUND THE WORLD
On hearing the news of Kennedy's death, Soviet premier Nikita Khrushchev and his wife immediately wired personal condolences to Mrs. Kennedy. In an unprecedented move, Soviet television broadcast live coverage, via satellite, of Kennedy's coffin arriving at the White House. The Soviet newspaper *Izvestia* covered the assassination on the front page, its coverage surpassing even the death of Franklin D. Roosevelt, the country's World War II ally.

At the majestic Cathedral of Notre Dame in Paris, a requiem mass was attended by Mrs. de Gaulle, Premier Georges Pompidou, and Ambassador and Mrs. Charles Bohlen of the United States. Similar memorials were held in capitals throughout Europe, including Madrid, Geneva, Athens, Bonn, Copenhagen, and Stockholm.

In London, the British Parliament made the unusual gesture of formally honoring Kennedy, a rare occurrence for a foreigner. Britons waited in long cues to sign condolence books at the American embassy.

In South Vietnam, two thousand students marched in Saigon to pay their respects to President Kennedy at the American embassy there.

BEYOND THE GRAVE
An ailing Joseph P. Kennedy, the family patriarch, learned of his son's death the day after it occurred. His caregiver and niece kept the news from him at the request of his family. Newspapers went undelivered and Senator Edward Kennedy pulled the wires from the back of his father's television set, making it inoperable. The patriarch was irritable about these inconveniences and, upon seeing his wife dressed in mourning, demanded an explanation. He was too frail and bereft to attend the services, and watched the mass on television in the company of Father John Cavanaugh.

Over the objections of her sister-in-law Ethel Kennedy, Jacqueline Kennedy had wanted a black border to surround the funeral mass card for guests at St. Matthew's. However, the cards, which were printed on very short notice using the only available press, located at the CIA facilities, were printed without borders and could not be reprinted in time for the service. Also, the First Lady had intended the card to say, "Dear God—please take care of your servant John Fitzgerald Kennedy. Please take him straight to heaven." Misunderstanding her instructions, Bobby Kennedy thought she had intended him to choose one or the other sentence, and so he omitted the second.

ODD COINCIDENCES
Eerie parallels can be drawn between John F. Kennedy's death and that of Abraham Lincoln: Lincoln's personal secretary was named Kennedy, and Kennedy's personal secretary was named Lincoln. They were elected one hundred years apart, in 1860 and 1960. Both were killed by an assassin's bullet. Both assassins had three names with fifteen characters—John Wilkes Booth and Lee Harvey Oswald.

SECRETS TO THE GRAVE

Two days after the assassination, Mrs. Kennedy composed a letter to her husband and asked her two children to compose notes to their father, although John could not write and Caroline could just barely write. Accompanied by Robert Kennedy, she gathered a pair of her husband's gold enameled cufflinks, a wedding gift from her, and a scrimshaw carved with the presidential seal that she had given her husband for Christmas, and with the three letters enclosed them in Kennedy's coffin. Robert took his PT-109 tie clip and a silver rosary given to him by his wife on their wedding day and placed them alongside his brother. They closed the casket for the final time.

BY THE NUMBERS

Kennedy was the sixth president to lie in state in the Capitol Rotunda. The others were Abraham Lincoln in April 1865, James A. Garfield in September 1881, William McKinley in September 1901, Warren G. Harding in August 1923, and William Howard Taft in March 1930. (Taft was chief justice at the time of his death.)

John F. Kennedy was the second president to be buried at Arlington National Cemetery. The twenty-seventh president, William Howard Taft, is buried near the entrance gate.

Kennedy was the fourth president to be assassinated. The others were Lincoln, in 1865, Garfield, in 1881, and McKinley, in 1901.

The day after Kennedy's funeral, Tuesday, November 26, 1963, saw the biggest one-day surge in the history of the stock market.

Three members of the Kennedy clan celebrated birthdays during the week of Kennedy's death and burial. Robert Kennedy celebrated his thirty-eighth birthday two days before his brother's death. John Jr.'s third birthday coincided with his father's funeral, and his sister, Caroline Kennedy, became six years old two days later, on November 27, 1963.

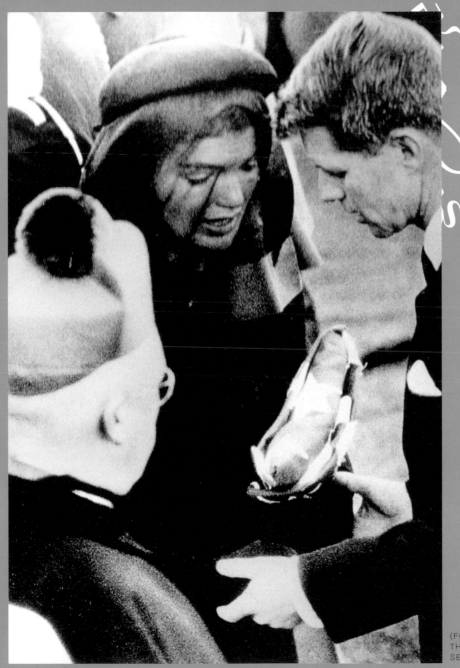

JACQUELINE KENNEDY, WITH CARDINAL CUSHING (FOREGROUND) AND ROBERT F. KENNEDY, CLASPS THE FLAG THAT HAD COVERED HER HUSBAND'S COFFIN AFTER GRAVESIDE SERVICES AT ARLINGTON NATIONAL CEMETERY.

AYATOLLAH KHOMEINI

"Imam"

May 17, 1900–June 3, 1989

"This is not a struggle between the United States and Iran. This is a struggle between Islam and blasphemy."

السلام عليك يا روح الله

THOUSANDS OF SHI'ITE MUSLIMS GATHER BENEATH A PORTRAIT OF THE IMAM, AT BEHESHT-E ZAHRA CEMETERY ON THE FORTY-DAY ANNIVERSARY OF **KHOMEINI**'S DEATH, JULY 13, 1989.

VITAL STATISTICS

AGE AT DEATH: 89

CAUSE OF DEATH: Heart failure twelve days after intestinal surgery

SURVIVOR: A son, Hojatolislam Ahmad Khomeini

LAST WORDS: In his last will and testament, read over Iranian radio, the Ayatollah denounced the government of the United States as "terrorists," saying, "May God's curse be upon them."

HIS LIFE

Details of the Ayatollah's early life, including the year and date of his birth, are difficult to confirm. It is known, however, that from his early childhood, Ruhollah Khomeini, the son and grandson of Shi'ite Muslim leaders, was immersed in religious training. Khomeini's father, an Ayatollah himself—a title of high Islamic spiritual honor, meaning "reflection of Allah"—was murdered over a dispute with a landlord while his son was still a boy. His mother and aunt ensured that the young man received religious tutoring, and he studied with a leading cleric in Qum, where he became a teacher himself. Ruhollah Khomeini developed an early interest in Islamic mysticism as well as in the teachings of Plato.

Khomeini married and had two children. His daughter died in childhood and his son died in the 1970s under mysterious circumstances, possibly involving the Shah's secret police. After his first wife died, Khomeini remarried and fathered three more daughters and a son.

Always at opposition with the more secular ruling family of Shahs who had come to power in the 1920s, Khomeini came to the Iranian public's attention with the 1941 publication of his book entitled *Unveiling the Mysteries,* which outlined his vision of a religiously structured Islamic republic. He also criticized the ruling regime of Shah Pahlevi for oppressing the clergy, encouraging foreign interests, and destroying the culture of Islam, themes he returned to again and again over the next thirty years.

In the 1950s, Khomeini's followers bestowed on him the title "Ayatollah," and he became the leader of the Shi'ite sect. By 1962, when the Shah was reinstated as Iran's head of state (after a nationalist coup had temporarily deposed him), Khomeini had earned the title "Grand Ayatollah," or Imam, a leader whose teachings are unquestioned. It was an honor shared by only five others in Iran.

By 1963, the Shah of Iran had taken steps to modernize Iran, including liberating women from Islamic codes and confiscating property owned by the clergy, steps vehemently opposed by Khomeini and his two hundred thousand fundamentalist supporters, many of whom were students. Khomeini's outspoken dissension soon led to his exile. In Turkey and later in Iraq, Khomeini kept in close contact with the mullahs who led opposition efforts in Iran, sending taped sermons denouncing Western influence and promoting a religious revolution to purify Iran.

In 1978, in response to an article criticizing Khomeini placed by the Shah in the state-controlled newspaper, outraged student followers of the religious leader held riotous demonstrations in major cities, which led to work strikes in the country's oil fields. In an attempt to restore order, the Shah offered amnesty to the Ayatollah, who refused to return until the Shah left Iran. The Shah retaliated by asking Iraq to expel Khomeini, which it did.

Settling in France, the Ayatollah built an international following of Muslims to overthrow the Pahlevi regime and, when the ailing Shah set up a provisional civilian government and left on holiday for Egypt in January 1979, Khomeini was ready. He returned to Iran on February 1, 1979, and within ten days he had replaced the provisional government and deposed the family that had ruled Iran for thirty-seven years.

Within months, Khomeini instituted Islamic fundamentalist restrictions, including the requirement that women wear the traditional body-covering *chadors* in public, and he ordered the killing of at least seven thousand people, including homosexuals, prostitutes, and political adversaries. Behavior in Iran was strictly prescribed, and punishment was severe. Soon thereafter Iraq invaded Iran, launching an eight-year territorial war that the Ayatollah said he would "fight to the last drop of my blood." An estimated million Iranians died in the war, which ended in a truce in 1988, despite the Ayatollah's rhetoric, with Iran in economic ruins but Khomeini still firmly in command.

Khomeini considered both the United States and the Soviet Union "Great Satans," and he relished the opportunity to humiliate President Jimmy Carter during a November 1979 takeover of the American embassy in Tehran by armed student revolutionaries. Claiming that he could not control the students, the Ayatollah let them hold fifty-two U.S. hostages for 444 days, releasing them the day President Ronald Reagan was sworn into office.

The Imam was in ailing health during much of 1989. Yet a few months before his death, the Ayatollah issued a decree calling for the death of the Indian-born British author Salman Rushdie, claiming that Rushdie's novel, *The Satanic Verses,* blasphemed against Islam. Khomeini offered a one-million-dollar bounty and promised ascension to heaven for any follower who suc-

ceeded in killing Rushdie, an offer finally rescinded publicly by the Iranian government nearly ten years after Khomeini's death. On Saturday, June 3, 1989, while recovering from stomach surgery, he suffered a heart attack and died.

BEST KNOWN FOR: Reasserting Shi'ite fundamentalism in Iran; the American hostage crisis; his fatwa demanding Salman Rushdie's death

FIRST JOB: Teacher

AVOCATION: Poetry

RITES OF PASSAGE

The eighty-three-member theological assembly in Iran selected President Hojatolislam Ali Khamenei to succeed Khomeini the day after he died, ensuring continued fundamentalist control of the country.

THE PREPARATION

By Monday, June 5, news of the Ayatollah's death had drawn hundreds of thousands of distraught mourners to a hill outside Tehran, where they had waited through the night to pay respects to their leader.

Khomeini's body was wrapped in a traditional white mourning cloth. That morning, bearers carried the body on a stretcher to a thirty-foot-high bier made from cargo containers draped in black. The Ayatollah remained on view in a refrigerated glass case with his black turban, signifying his link to the prophet Muhammad, resting on his chest.

PAYING RESPECTS

Hundreds of thousands of devout Muslims prayed, chanted, and wept at the bier. Iranian newscasters, reporting live on state television, cried on camera.

Eight people were crushed to death and more than five hundred were injured as the hysterical crowd pushed to get close to the Ayatollah's body. In the one-hundred-degree heat many were overcome and fainted. Fire hoses sprayed on the mob provided the only relief from the heat.

Dignitaries had difficulty reaching the bier and many rode in helicopters hovering above the glass-enclosed body. Women sat in clusters under their black chadors chanting and weeping while holding large photographs of the Imam. Families held their children and babies aloft to be passed overhead for a view of the man who had led them. Distraught men beat their heads and chests, crying out in the traditional Shi'ite practice of mourning.

THE FUNERAL

On Tuesday, June 6, in front of a crowd of an estimated three million mourners, the Ayatollah Khomeini was given funeral rites, but not before his anguished followers wreaked havoc over the twelve-mile processional route. Crowds surged in order to glimpse the religious leader's body. Several mourners died in the crush. The exact numbers are unknown, but journalists reported that at least eleven thousand people were injured during the funeral. Tuesday's heat reached one hundred degrees and again water hoses cooled the crowds, who chanted, "We have lost our father," and "Death to America."

The state considered postponing the funeral because the frenzied mob seemed uncontrollable. The density of the crowds prevented the passage of a refrigerated truck carrying the Ayatollah's body from the place where the body had lain in state to the burial site at Behesht-e Zahra cemetery, the "cemetery of martyrs." The Ayatollah's coffin was ultimately transferred to an army helicopter for transport.

When the helicopter landed at the burial site, members of the Revolutionary Guards, on duty to maintain order, paraded the coffin high overhead. Mourners grabbed wildly at Khomeini's coffin, pulling it open and exposing the Ayatollah, rending his shroud and pulling their beloved patriarch to the ground. Broadcast live on television, the images of Iran's most revered cleric toppling half-nude into a sea of frenetic mourners shocked the watching world. Soldiers quickly recovered the body to the safety of a helicopter, but distraught members of the crowd clutched the helicopter, temporarily preventing its liftoff. Several mourners threw themselves into the open grave.

FINAL RESTING PLACE Soldiers eventually restored order at Behesht-e Zahra cemetery. When they were finally able to proceed, three military helicopters formed the cortege. The first bore Hojatolislam Hashemi Rafsanjani, the Speaker of the Parliament; the second carried other religious leaders; the third held the Ayatollah's son, Hojatolislam Ahmad Khomeini, and the body of Iran's deceased leader encased in a metal cargo box. As the Ayatollah was removed from the helicopter, the crowds again swelled, but soldiers maintained order. Nine hours behind schedule, the shroud-wrapped Ayatollah Ruhollah Khomeini was buried, without a coffin in a shallow grave, in keeping with Muslim custom.

Ten years earlier, at the same cemetery on the south side of Tehran, the Ayatollah had delivered his homecoming speech after nearly twenty years of exile, promising that Iran would "cut off the hands" of its enemies.

NEWS OF THE DAY

JUNE 4, 1989

TROOPS ATTACK AND CRUSH BEIJING PROTEST; THOUSANDS FIGHT BACK, SCORES ARE KILLED

KHOMEINI, IMAM OF IRAN AND FOE OF U.S., IS DEAD

BEYOND THE GRAVE

After the Ayatollah's death, a *ghazal,* or love poem, that he had written to honor the daughter of Muhammad, was printed in Iranian newspapers, startling some with its open sensuality. The poem begins, "I have become imprisoned, O beloved, by the mole on your lip! I saw your ailing eyes and became ill through love."

Khomeini graced the January 7, 1980, cover of *Time* as the magazine's 1979 "Man of the Year."

ODD COINCIDENCES

The helicopter that carried the Speaker of the Parliament to the cemetery was an American-supplied Huey, a leftover from the Shah's regime.

The religious leader of the Shi'ite sect and the Roman Catholic Pope John XXIII died on the same day, June 3, separated by twenty-six years.

MEMORIALS AND TRIBUTES

In 1991, Iran opened a shrine dedicated to the Ayatollah Khomeini. Located at the cemetery Behesht-e Zahra, the shrine is the first modern structure to a deceased Imam. In keeping with the style of shrines of the great Imams in the Islamic holy cities in Iraq and Saudi Arabia, the new shrine rests on columns that support a golden dome and minarets, but it is constructed of modern concrete and steel materials.

The Ayatollah's shrine has become a new destination for pilgrimages and its inviting interior is open to families and foreign visitors in addition to the truly devout. Underneath a crystal chandelier in the center of a marbled interior, a silver cage surrounds the maroon-colored marble tomb of Khomeini. Hand-woven rugs scattered about provide a place for visitors to eat their lunch in the shadow of Khomeini's crypt.

MOURNERS EAGER TO TOUCH THE BODY OF THE
AYATOLLAH KHOMEINI PULL OPEN HIS COFFIN AS IT IS
PASSED OVERHEAD EN ROUTE TO BEHESHT-E ZAHRA CEMETERY.

MARTIN LUTHER KING JR.

"Doc"

January 15, 1929–April 4, 1968

"If a man hasn't found something he will die for, he isn't fit to live."

↬ A MEMORIAL BUTTON.

VITAL STATISTICS

AGE AT DEATH: 39

CAUSE OF DEATH: Gunshot wound from an assassin's bullet

SURVIVORS: His wife, Coretta Scott King; two sons, Martin and Dexter; two daughters, Yolanda and Bernice; a brother, Rev. A. D. Williams King; a sister, Christine King Farris; and his parents, Rev. Martin Luther King Sr. and Alberta Williams King

CLOSE CALLS: On September 20, 1958, King was stabbed in the chest while signing copies of his first book, *Stride Toward Freedom,* in Harlem. He underwent surgery and was on the critical list for several days.

HIS LIFE

Martin Luther King Jr., born Michael Luther King Jr., was the first son and second child of a middle-class Atlanta, Georgia, couple, the Reverend Michael Luther King and his wife Alberta. When his son was five years old, Rev. King changed his and his son's given name to Martin in honor of the sixteenth-century theologian and reformer, Martin Luther.

The young King performed well in his segregated public high school, skipping grades and graduating at age fifteen. In 1944, the teenager entered Morehouse College in Atlanta, where he hoped to forge a career in medicine or law, majoring in sociology but unsure of which career path to follow. However, aware of his gift for oratory, King wanted to put it to good use and ultimately, decided to pursue his father's vocation instead.

King graduated in 1948 and presently entered Crozer Theological Seminary in Chester, Pennsylvania, where he studied philosophy, theology, ethics, and the teachings of Mahatma Gandhi, who had been assassinated earlier that year. Enthralled with Gandhi's philosophy of nonviolence, King immersed himself in the Indian leader's teachings.

After graduating at the top of his class from Crozer, King attended Boston University, where he pursued his doctoral work in systemic theology. There he met Coretta Scott, a graduate of Antioch College who was studying voice at the New England Conservatory of Music. The couple married in 1953 and a year later King accepted his own ministry at a small parish in Montgomery, Alabama. He received his doctorate in philosophy in 1955 and henceforth was known as Dr. King.

Montgomery, one of the most segregated cities in the South, attracted national attention on December 1, 1955, when an African American woman named Rosa Parks was jailed for her refusal to give up her bus seat to a white passenger. The local chapter of the National Association for the Advancement of Colored People (NAACP) called upon religious and community leaders to support a one-day boycott of the Montgomery bus system. A newly formed protest group, the Montgomery Improvement Association, called the eloquent, twenty-six-year-old King to act as its spokesperson.

Black citizens of Montgomery refused to ride the city bus line for 381 consecutive days, sending its private operator into bankruptcy. On December 21, 1956, the U.S. Supreme Court ordered Montgomery to integrate its bus line. The protesters began to gain national exposure for their cause to end segregation, and the charismatic Dr. King became a focal point in the civil rights movement.

King practiced Gandhi's principle of *satyagraha* (holding to the truth) in the form of nonviolent disobedience. In 1957, Dr. King's Montgomery home and church were bombed. That same year, with Rev. Ralph Abernathy, he helped form the Southern Christian Leadership Conference (SCLC) to work toward ending inequality. King traveled and lectured widely, appeared at rallies, and published his first book, *Stride Toward Freedom,* in 1958. In the early 1960s, King helped organize nonviolent activism that spawned voter-registration drives, rallies to integrate interstate bus terminals, and sit-ins at lunch counters.

When local leaders in Birmingham, Alabama, invited Dr. King to help them organize protests in their segregated city, he and his SCLC colleagues rose to the challenge. In April 1963, Dr. King and Rev. Abernathy were joined by thousands of courageous men, women, and children in a nonviolent march. They were greeted by police brandishing billy clubs, high-power water hoses, and attack dogs. Seeing these shocking images on television helped persuade many more people to join the civil rights cause.

Disobeying an ordinance preventing further protests, King and Abernathy took to the streets again; they were arrested and jailed for five days. During his period of solitary confinement, Dr. King wrote a nine-thousand-word manifesto on scraps of newspaper, later published as *Letter from a Birmingham Jail,* eloquently detailing his civil rights philosophy. The incarceration at Birmingham was one of twenty arrests King endured in his fight for equality.

The SCLC, under King's direction, organized the enormous March on Washington, D.C., in August 1963. Two hundred and fifty thousand people came from all parts of the country to march from the Washington Monument to the Lincoln Memorial, calling for civil rights legislation and an immediate end to segregation. On the steps of the Lincoln Memorial, singers Marian

Anderson; Mahalia Jackson; Peter, Paul, and Mary; Joan Baez; and Bob Dylan performed, and entertainers such as Sammy Davis Jr., Ossie Davis, Harry Belafonte, Lena Horne, and Josephine Baker spoke on the cause of equality. From the steps of the memorial, King gave his most memorable speech, including the words that have forever since been associated with him, *"I have a dream . . ."*

In January 1964, *Time* magazine selected Martin Luther King Jr. as its 1963 "Man of the Year," the first black man to receive that honor. In October of that same year, the Nobel Prize Committee awarded Dr. King the Nobel Peace Prize. At thirty-five years old, Martin Luther King Jr. was the youngest person ever to have received the Nobel commendation.

In the mid-1960s, the SCLC concentrated on drives to register black voters in the South and end discriminatory voting tests and taxes. The U.S. Congress passed the Voting Rights Act in 1965 in response to the SCLC protests.

By the late 1960s, discord had developed within the black community as urban, militant members, unhappy with the slow pace of the nonviolent movement, supported more radical tactics endorsed by the popular Muslim leader Malcolm X. Meanwhile, King broadened his efforts to gain economic and social justice. In 1967, he and the SCLC began planning a multiracial protest, billed as the Poor People's Campaign, to call for an end to all forms of discrimination. That same year, Dr. King spoke out against the Johnson administration's policies in the ongoing Vietnam War, advocating a peace settlement.

While crossing the country in March 1968 to raise money for the campaign, striking sanitation workers in Memphis asked King to speak at a rally on behalf of their cause for higher wages and better working conditions. Beset by problems from the beginning, the march was postponed because of a snowstorm, and the rescheduled event on March 28, which he did not attend, ended in violence, leaving one person dead. King vowed to lead a nonviolent protest in response. He flew to Memphis on April 3, 1968, and delivered a moving speech that evening to an audience of five hundred.

The next evening, an assassin shot Martin Luther King Jr. in the neck as he stood on the balcony of his motel, speaking to the Reverend Jesse Jackson, who was standing in the parking lot below. He was taken to St. Joseph's Hospital where, after emergency-room efforts failed to save him, he died at 7:05 P.M. central time.

In spite of an extensive manhunt, the assassin, later identified as James Earl Ray, escaped capture. He was subsequently apprehended in England, extradited, and convicted of King's murder.

BEST KNOWN FOR: His tireless commitment to the civil rights movement; his stirring orations
FIRST JOB: Preacher
AVOCATION: Writing

RITES OF PASSAGE

King's assassination, just four and a half years after the death of President John F. Kennedy, shocked the country. President Johnson spoke on national television shortly after receiving news of King's murder, asking that "every citizen reject the blind violence that has struck Dr. King, who lived by nonviolence." The nation's black community experienced a grief unequaled in modern time, and they took to the streets in both anger and sorrow. Riots erupted in communities including Newark, New Jersey; Washington, D.C.; Baltimore, Maryland; Hartford, Connecticut; Memphis, Tennessee; Jackson,

Mississippi; and Los Angeles, California. The National Guard was called in to restore peace in many urban centers. The looting and rioting quickly eclipsed the nonviolent principles that King had worked so hard to promote. In order to stem the violence, many cities, including the nation's capital, established curfews requiring all citizens to be inside by early evening or face arrest.

THE PREPARATION

In a jet chartered by Senator Robert F. Kennedy, Dr. Martin Luther King Jr.'s body was returned home to Atlanta in a bronze casket accompanied by Dr. King's family and friends: Mrs. King; Rev. King's brother, Rev. A. D. Williams King; Rev. Ralph Abernathy; and Rev. Andrew Young. In Atlanta, Mrs. King was met by her four children and a host of dignitaries headed by family friend and Atlanta mayor Ivan Allen Jr. A hearse transported King's body to the Hanley Funeral Home in northeast Atlanta in preparation for the public viewing and funeral service.

PAYING RESPECTS

President Johnson declared Sunday, April 7, a national day of mourning, and canceled a trip to Hawaii during which he had planned to meet with military and diplomatic advisers regarding Vietnam. A memorial service was held on Friday, April 5, at the National Cathedral in Washington, D.C., where Dr. King had preached only five days earlier. President Johnson, Vice President Humphrey, all the members of the Supreme Court and the Cabinet, and four thousand others attended the service. An organist played "We Shall Overcome" as a processional dirge, and later a children's choir sang the song as the congregation recessed.

In New York, a peaceful multiracial gathering began in Central Park and proceeded down Broadway to City Hall. Flags flew at half-staff all along Fifth

Avenue and many businesses and schools closed. And longshoremen closed ports from Maine to Florida in memory of Dr. King, a tribute whose only precedent was the interruption of port traffic for the memorial of President Kennedy in 1963.

All around the country, citizens showed their respect for Martin Luther King Jr. In Madison, Wisconsin, twenty thousand people walked two miles in silent tribute. In Austin, Texas, five thousand students attended a memorial service and then marched to the state capitol to call for an end to discrimination at the University of Texas. In Memphis, clergy representing Protestants, Catholics, and Jews participated in a silent memorial march through the center of town. Marches, ceremonies, and tributes were held in cities across the United States as people grieved the loss of the great leader.

On Sunday, April 7, Rev. A. D. King, Martin Luther's younger brother, delivered a sermon at Atlanta's Ebenezer Baptist Church entitled "Why America May Go to Hell." The two-hour service featured a moving performance of "Nobody Knows the Trouble I've Seen" by Mahalia Jackson, the gifted gospel singer, and renowned jazz trumpeter Dizzy Gillespie.

Also on Sunday, Dr. King's body lay in state in an open casket in the Sister's Chapel at Spelman College in Atlanta. Dr. King's bronze casket had been exchanged for one of African mahogany at the Atlanta funeral home. Upon seeing his son laid out, Rev. Martin Luther King Sr. collapsed in tears at the chapel.

Public viewing began at 6:30 P.M. and continued until 4:30 P.M. on Monday, April 8, when the body was transferred to Ebenezer Baptist Church in preparation for Tuesday's funeral. Dr. King also lay in state there, where as an ordained teenager he had served his father as assistant pastor. Senator and Mrs. Robert F. Kennedy and thousands of others paid their respects late

Monday evening. An estimated sixty thousand mourners filed passed Dr. King's coffin.

On Monday, April 8, Mrs. King returned to the city of her husband's murder to take his place in a march for the sanitation workers' union. Accompanied by her three oldest children, Mrs. King marched at the front of thousands of peaceful demonstrators. She was joined by singer Harry Belafonte, actor Ossie Davis, and pediatrician Dr. Benjamin Spock, all of whom spoke at a City Hall tribute later in the day. Hundreds of mourners gathered at United Nations Plaza in New York for two separate ceremonies honoring Dr. King.

Although not a federally mandated holiday, many states and municipalities closed schools, businesses, and nonessential services for most or part of the day of Dr. King's funeral, Tuesday, April 9, with the exception of Georgia, King's home state, where segregationist Governor Lester G. Maddux refused to close schools for the day.

THE FUNERAL

THE SERVICE Rev. Dr. Martin Luther King Jr.'s funeral took place Tuesday, April 9, at Ebenezer Baptist Church, where he had so often delivered sermons. King's coffin, closed for the service, rested at the base of the pulpit, blanketed in white lilies, chrysanthemums, and roses. A white floral cross stood nearby. The service had been scheduled to begin at 10:30 A.M., but grieving members of the public who had gathered outside the church since five o'clock that morning made it difficult for guests to enter.

The thirteen-hundred-seat church filled rapidly with political notables, among them Vice President Hubert Humphrey; Supreme Court justice Thurgood Marshall; Governor Nelson Rockefeller of New York; Governor George Romney of Michigan; Attorney General Ramsey Clark; former vice

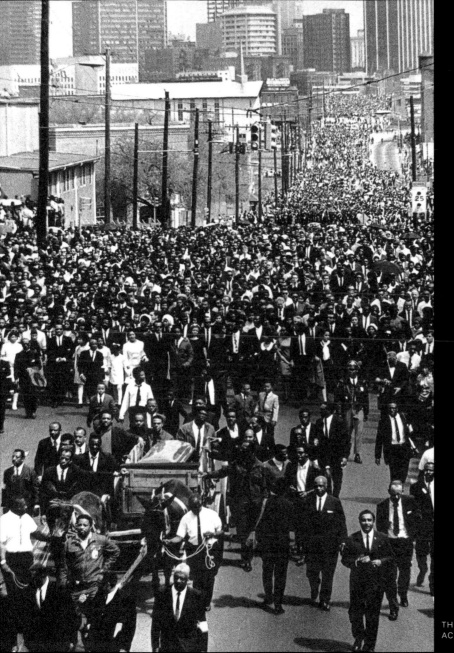

A MULE-DRAWN WAGON CARRIES **KING**'S BODY ON THREE-MILE JOURNEY THROUGH THE STREETS OF ATLANTA, ACCOMPANIED BY MORE THAN 50,000 MOURNERS.

president Richard M. Nixon; Ralph Bunche, undersecretary of the United Nations; and Arthur Goldberg, U.S. ambassador to the United Nations. Among the thirty senators and fifty congressmen in attendance were Robert F. Kennedy, Edward M. Kennedy, Jacob K. Javits, and Eugene J. McCarthy. Mayors of many cities, including Ivan Allen of Atlanta and John V. Lindsay of New York, also attended the funeral rites. Black activist Stokeley Carmichael caused a disturbance when he arrived with six bodyguards who had not been invited to the service. Notably absent was Governor Lester G. Maddux, who had stationed himself across town in the state capitol building.

Celebrities attending the service included singers Harry Belafonte, Aretha Franklin, Diana Ross and the Supremes, Eartha Kitt, Mahalia Jackson, and Sammy Davis Jr.; actors Marlon Brando and Bill Cosby; and sports legends Jackie Robinson and Floyd Patterson. Mrs. John F. Kennedy, who had visited Mrs. King and her four children earlier that morning at the King home, was mobbed by the throng and had to be forcibly pulled into the church.

The well-meaning but oppressive crowds continued to delay the commencement of the funeral. On two occasions Dr. King's brother stood on a car to plead with the mob, which had swelled to thirty-five thousand, to allow his family into the church. Finally, he said, "If we can't receive your cooperation, we have but one choice to remove the body and bury it privately."

At 10:43 A.M. the funeral began with a greeting by Rev. Ralph Abernathy, who called Dr. King's assassination "one of the darkest hours of mankind." The traditional Southern Baptist service was peppered with music, assisted by the 160 voices of the Ebenezer choir. Abernathy opened with a prayer and the Twenty-third Psalm, followed by two hymns, "When I Survey the Wondrous Cross" and "In Christ There Is No East or West." The congregation joined the choir in singing the gospel song "Softly and Tenderly."

At Mrs. King's request, taped portions of a sermon her husband had delivered in his last appearance at Ebenezer Baptist Church were played for the audience. The lyrical, powerful sound of Dr. King's voice brought tears:

> *". . . if you're around when I have to meet my day, I don't want a long funeral. And if you get somebody to deliver the eulogy, tell him not to talk too long . . . Tell him not to mention that I have a Nobel Peace Prize—that isn't important . . . I'd like somebody to mention that day that Martin Luther King Jr. tried to love somebody . . . I want you to be able to say that day that I did try to feed the hungry. I want you to say that I tried to love and serve humanity."*

Following the hymn "Where He Leads Me," Abernathy closed the service with a spiritual often quoted by King, "I Shall Not Have Died in Vain," and a reading of the first line of the Twenty-third Psalm, "The Lord is my shepherd." He then led the procession out of the church.

THE PROCESSION Dr. King's funeral procession led from Ebenezer Baptist Church to downtown Atlanta and finished three and a half miles away at Morehouse College. In the afternoon heat, several mourners fainted along the route. Dr. King's elegant mahogany casket was placed atop a wooden farm carriage pulled by two mules. Thousands of mourners marched silently through the streets behind this symbol of poverty and simple rural life.

At Morehouse, the push of the crowd again delayed the start of the open-air service, which began an hour later than scheduled. Dozens fainted during the tribute. Due to the lateness of the hour and the fact that so many mourners had suffered heat sickness, Rosa Parks, Atlanta's mayor Ivan Allen Jr., and the Most Reverend James Wright, the Roman Catholic bishop of Pittsburgh, never delivered their speeches.

A hearse transported Dr. King's coffin to South View Cemetery, founded in 1866, on the outskirts of Atlanta, where Martin Luther King Jr.'s grandparents were buried. The four-mile route from Morehouse College to the cemetery was also lined with thousands of mourners. Rev. Abernathy delivered graveside prayers: "The cemetery is too small for his spirit, but we submit his body to the ground. The grave is too narrow for his soul, but we commit his body to the ground. No coffin, no crypt, no stone can hold his greatness. But we submit his body to the ground."

FINAL RESTING PLACE The civil rights leader's body is now entombed in an above-ground marble grave in the center of Freedom Plaza in central Atlanta, surrounded by the 23-acre Martin Luther King Jr. National Historical Site. The epitaph on his gravestone, taken from a Black spiritual says, "Free at last; free at last; thank God Almighty I'm free at last."

NEWS OF THE DAY
APRIL 5, 1968
MARTIN LUTHER KING IS SLAIN IN MEMPHIS;
A WHITE IS SUSPECTED; JOHNSON URGES CALM

DISMAY IN NATION

PRESIDENT'S PLEA

GUARD CALLED OUT

SCATTERED VIOLENCE OCCURS IN HARLEM AND BROOKLYN

HANOI CHARGES U.S. RAID
FAR NORTH OF 20TH PARALLEL

APRIL 6, 1968
ARMY TROOPS IN CAPITAL AS NEGROES RIOT;
GUARD SENT INTO CHICAGO, DETROIT, BOSTON;
JOHNSON ASKS A JOINT SESSION OF CONGRESS

7 DIE AS FIRES AND LOOTING SPREAD IN CHICAGO RIOTING

EUROPE DISMAYED; FEARFUL FOR U.S.

CLARK IS SURE KILLER WILL BE SOON SEIZED

APRIL 8, 1968
U.S. TROOPS SENT TO BALTIMORE;
VIOLENCE EASES IN PITTSBURGH;
DR. KING MOURNED IN THE NATION

MRS. KING TO MARCH IN HUSBAND'S PLACE IN MEMPHIS TODAY

WASHINGTON TURMOIL SUBSIDES;
HUNDREDS HOMELESS, EIGHT DEAD

DR. KING'S ASSASSIN ON RUN, CLARK SAYS

SOVIET FIRES ROCKET;
MOON ORBIT LIKELY

APRIL 10, 1968
DR. MARTIN LUTHER KING BURIED IN ATLANTA;
A VAST CORTEGE FOLLOWS MULE-DRAWN BIER

ATLANTA IS PEACEFUL DURING THE FUNERAL

AN ATLANTA SHOE STORE IS CLOSED TO HONOR **MARTIN LUTHER KING JR.** ON THE DAY OF HIS FUNERAL.

OTHER DEATHS

By the day of Dr. King's funeral, violent outbreaks set off by his assassination had claimed the lives of at least twenty-nine people: eleven died in Chicago, eight in Washington, D.C., four in Baltimore, two in Detroit, and one each in Memphis, Minneapolis, Newark, and Tallahassee.

A year after Dr. King's death, his brother, A. D. King, died in a drowning accident. Five years later, in 1974, King's mother was shot and killed while playing the organ at the Ebenezer Baptist Church.

AROUND THE WORLD

European nations struggled to make sense of the recent violence in the United States while lamenting the loss of Dr. King. Britain's Parliament introduced motions deploring King's death and pledged to eliminate racial discrimination. Headlines in Spain read "America Again Under Terror." Pope Paul VI, who had met Dr. King in 1964, released a prayerful statement.

African nations such as Nigeria and Tanzania released compassionate statements while both whites and blacks in South Africa, a nation under apartheid, waited in long lines to read special-edition newspaper reports of Dr. King's killing.

BEYOND THE GRAVE
ODD COINCIDENCES

On the night before he was murdered, acknowledging that he had received death threats upon arriving in Memphis, King delivered an inspirational speech with hopeful visions of the future:

"We've got some difficult days ahead. But it really doesn't matter with me now. Because I've been to the mountaintop. I won't mind. Like anybody, I would like to live a long life. Longevity has its place. But I'm not concerned about that now. I just want to do God's will. And he's allowed me to go up to the mountain. And I've looked over, and I've seen the Promised Land. I may not get there with you, but I want you to know tonight that we as a people will get to the Promised Land. So I'm happy tonight. I'm not worried about anything. I'm not fearing any man. Mine eyes have seen the glory of the coming of the Lord."

SECRETS TO THE GRAVE

In 1990, scholars discovered that portions of King's doctoral thesis contained sections plagiarized from the work of philosopher and theologian Paul Tillich and that of a fellow student, Jack Boozer.

The Federal Bureau of Investigation (FBI), under the leadership of J. Edgar Hoover, eavesdropped on Martin Luther King Jr. and his colleagues at the SCLC, hoping to discredit him by uncovering personal indiscretions or ties to groups the FBI did not like.

In 1989, Rev. Ralph Abernathy, King's right-hand man and successor, wrote an autobiography, *And the Walls Came Tumbling Down,* in which he exposed personal information about Martin Luther King Jr., which many felt was unkind and indefensible.

MYSTERIOUS CIRCUMSTANCES

Although James Earl Ray was arrested, convicted, and jailed for the assassination of Dr. King, members of the King family subscribe to a conspiracy theory promoted by Ray and his lawyer, William Pepper. In 1999, a year after Ray died in prison, the King family won a civil suit against a bar owner who claimed involvement in the murder of Dr. King. At the request of the family, the Justice Department conducted an eighteen-month investigation, ending in June 2000, which found no evidence of a plot, plan, or conspiracy to assassinate King and concurred with the 1969 Justice Department report. Nevertheless, the King family and their supporters, using some of the FBI's own files to bolster their case, still cling to their belief that James Earl Ray did not act alone.

MEMORIALS AND TRIBUTES

The U.S. Congress made Martin Luther King Jr.'s birthday a federal holiday in 1986. No other twentieth-century American has been honored with a federal holiday.

In 1999, the National Capital Planning Commission finally approved a memorial to Dr. King to be erected in Washington, D.C., on four acres across from the Jefferson Memorial. Dr. King's fraternity, Alpha Phi Alpha, organized the design competition and raised funds for the construction, which is expected to begin in 2003.

MARILYN MONROE

"The Blonde Bombshell"

June 1, 1926–August 5, 1962

"I was never used to being happy, so that wasn't something I ever took for granted."

↬ **MONROE**, ON THE SET OF HER LAST COMPLETED FILM *THE MISFITS*.

VITAL STATISTICS

AGE AT DEATH: 36

CAUSE OF DEATH: Barbiturate poisoning, presumed a suicide

SURVIVORS: Her institutionalized mother, Gladys Baker Eley; and a half-sister, Bernice Miracle

CLOSE CALLS: Several suicide attempts in connection with bouts of depression

LAST WORDS: "I think we'll not go to the beach tomorrow for a ride" (spoken to her housekeeper before Monroe retired for the evening).

HER LIFE

Born Norma Jean Mortenson in Los Angeles to an unwed mother, abandonment and tragedy were key themes in Marilyn Monroe's childhood. When she was three years old, her estranged father died in a motorcycle accident. Her uncle later committed suicide. Her mother and maternal grandparents were frequently dispatched to mental institutions. In between her mother's asylum incarcerations, Norma Jean was farmed out to at least ten foster homes and she eventually eschewed her father's name, taking her mother's surname, Baker. Before starring in films, she earned a living as a model. In the late 1940s, after signing a contract with Twentieth Century Fox, the studio changed her name to Marilyn Monroe.

Monroe's break came in 1949 with a bit part in the Marx Brothers' movie *Love Happy,* followed by two small but significant roles in 1950, in *The Asphalt Jungle* and *All About Eve.* She performed in eleven more films before hitting outright celebrity status, after costarring with Jane Powell in 1953's *Gentlemen Prefer Blondes.* That role, as a sweet and sensual, but not very bright, gold digger was forever linked with Monroe.

In light comedy roles she combined an overpowering sensuality with a youthful vulnerability that transformed her into a box-office sensation in such films as *How to Marry a Millionaire* (1953), *The Seven-Year Itch* (1955), *Bus Stop* (1956), *Some Like It Hot* (1959), and *Let's Make Love* (1960). She graced the cover of every major magazine. Representing the ideal of American female sexuality, Monroe notably appeared on the cover of *Playboy* magazine's inaugural issue in December 1953.

Her last completed film, *The Misfits* (1960), costarring Clark Gable, directed by John Huston, and written by her third husband, playwright Arthur Miller, finally showcased her talent as a dramatic actress. By this time, however, Monroe's dependence on sleeping pills and her erratic work schedule finally unraveled her career. In 1962, she was fired from her final film project, *Something's Got to Give.*

Peace eluded Marilyn Monroe offscreen, and she never seemed to find the love she sought so desperately. She was only sixteen when she married James Dougherty, a factory worker, and twenty when she divorced. Her marriage to baseball legend Joe DiMaggio did not survive a full year, although they remained friends and were in contact in the weeks prior to her death. She was married to Arthur Miller for four years, suffering debilitating miscarriages during their union. The tabloid press followed Monroe's every move, linking her romantically with numerous celebrities. In 1962, at New York's Madison Square Garden, her seductive rendition of "Happy Birthday," addressed to President Kennedy, fueled rumors of affairs with both the chief executive and his brother, Bobby. Even though she reportedly earned $200 million for the studios, friends have reported that Monroe never felt accepted by Hollywood or her peers. Her public image masked her mood swings, depressions, and loneliness.

Versions of Monroe's death differ on several points, but is generally agreed that at three o'clock in the morning on August 5, 1962, the housekeeper knocked on the bedroom door of Monroe's home in Brentwood, California, and, receiving no response, went to the garden to peer through the window. She saw Marilyn Monroe sprawled naked and motionless on the bed and called the star's psychoanalyst. In the official version, police were not called to Monroe's house until the analyst, Dr. Ralph Greenson, and her physician arrived and confirmed that the star was dead.

BEST KNOWN FOR: Her sex appeal and breathy whisper
FIRST JOB: Model
AVOCATION: Reading

RITES OF PASSAGE

THE PREPARATION

The Los Angeles County Coroner's Office performed an autopsy before releasing Monroe's body on Monday, August 6, to the Westwood Village Mortuary. Monroe's second husband, Joe DiMaggio, took charge of the private service, denying access to the media and limiting attendance to a few close friends and relatives. Asked to compose a eulogy, Carl Sandburg, the renowned American poet, declined because of illness.

THE FUNERAL

Fewer than thirty-five people attended Monroe's funeral services on Wednesday, August 8, 1962, at Westwood Memorial Park Chapel, the rustic church adjacent to the mortuary. Guests included publicist Pat Newcomb, with whom Monroe had spent her last day; Actors' Studio founders Lee and Paula Strasberg; and their daughter, Susan Strasberg, Monroe's close friend.

The thirty-six-year-old star's champagne-velvet-lined, bronze coffin was open and, for her final appearance, she wore a green jersey dress with no jewelry or embellishments except a bouquet of miniature pink roses that DiMaggio had placed in her hands.

THE SERVICE Although Monroe had converted to Judaism upon her marriage to Miller, the Reverend A. J. Soldan presided over the nondenominational service, which included readings of the Twenty-third, Forty-ninth, and One-hundred-thirty-ninth Psalms. Music selected for the service included Tchaikovsky's "Andante Cantabile" from his Sixth Symphony, *Pathétique,* and "Over the Rainbow," from the movie *The Wizard of Oz.* Lee Strasberg delivered the brief eulogy, describing his former student as "a warm human being, impulsive, shy, sensitive, and in fear of rejection, yet ever avid for life and reaching out for fulfillment."

At the conclusion of the service, DiMaggio kissed his former bride, saying, "I love you, I love you," before the casket was permanently sealed. Accompanied by his son, Joe DiMaggio Jr., the Yankee Clipper wept openly during the brief walk from the chapel to the mortuary.

FINAL RESTING PLACE Burial followed the short service in the adjoining Westwood Village Mortuary Cemetery. It was eerily quiet. The mobs of adoring fans that had been expected to storm the Westwood chapel did not materialize.

Every year afterward on the anniversary of her death, Joe DiMaggio placed a single red rose at her crypt.

NEWS OF THE DAY

AUGUST 6, 1962

MARILYN MONROE DEAD, PILLS NEAR

KENNEDY PRESSES FOR SAFER DRUGS

*RUSSIANS RESUME
A-TESTING IN AIR BLAST
2D BIGGEST*

AROUND THE WORLD

In Russia, the newspaper *Izvestia* treated Monroe in death more sympathetically than it had during her life, concluding, "Marilyn Monroe was a victim of Hollywood . . . that appalling monster that mocks art, kindness, sincerity, naturalness."

BEYOND THE GRAVE

Monroe joked that her epitaph would read *"Here lies Marilyn Monroe — 38-23-36."* In fact her crypt reads simply "Marilyn Monroe 1926–1962."

Speculating in an interview about what death might be like, she said, "It might be kind of a relief to be finished. It's sort of like, I don't know what kind of yard dash you're running, but then you're at the finish line and you sort of sigh—you've made it! But you never have—you have to start all over again."

Hollywood rat pack luminaries Frank Sinatra, Dean Martin, and Peter Lawford had expected to receive invitations to Monroe's funeral but did not. When DiMaggio shut them out, the *Los Angeles Times* quoted a disgruntled Lawford, "It seems to be a concerted effort to keep some of Marilyn's old friends from attending. I don't know why."

MYSTERIOUS CIRCUMSTANCES

Debate continues over whether Monroe took an accidental overdose, committed suicide, or was murdered. Fans have speculated that because only trace chemicals were found in her stomach and liver, a murderer could have administered a Nembutal enema.

THE HEREAFTER

In 1990, Marilyn Monroe's estate estimated that the licensing of her name and image had generated far more money than she had earned in her lifetime. As of the thirtieth anniversary of the star's death, the estate's licensing agency was receiving twenty requests each week for the use of her likeness in connection with dolls, calendars, eyeglasses, and even wine. The estate has rejected proposals for feminine napkins and toilet tissue.

NOTORIOUS B.I.G.

"Biggie Smalls"

May 21, 1972–March 9, 1997

"I spit phrases that'll thrill you.
You're nobody 'til somebody kills you."

⌇ A FRONT PAGE TRIBUTE TO THE MURDERED RAPPER.

VITAL STATISTICS

AGE AT DEATH: 24
CAUSE OF DEATH: Gunshot wound from an assassin's bullet
SURVIVORS: His estranged wife, Faith Evans; a son,
                      Christopher Jr.; a daughter, T'yanna, from a
                      previous relationship; his girlfriend, Lil' Kim;
                      and his mother, Voletta Wallace

HIS LIFE

At 6 feet 3 inches tall and close to three hundred pounds, "the Notorious B.I.G.," also known as "Biggie Smalls," was a gangsta-rap superstar. A high-school dropout raised by his mother in Brooklyn, the performer then known as Christopher Wallace rapped about his world of drugs, guns, and easy women. The Notorious B.I.G occasionally displayed a violent temper and had been arrested for assault just months before his death. Both a product and an escapee of his childhood neighborhood, he settled in suburban Teaneck, New Jersey, after achieving stardom.

The Notorious B.I.G. had not originally intended to become a professional rapper. However, fate interceded when friends forwarded amateur recordings that he had made with a local group to the music magazine *The Source*. His rapping was reviewed in the publication's "Unsigned Hype" column, and Biggie's career was born.

Although a compilation album to which he had been invited to contribute by *The Source* never became reality, a recording contract with A&R's Uptown did, and the Notorious B.I.G. changed from local 'hood celebrity to gangsta-rap recording star within weeks. Under the tutelage of Uptown's national director, Sean "Puffy" Combs, B.I.G. first performed on albums with established artists Mary J. Blige and Jodeci before signing a solo record deal.

Biggie was just twenty-one when he cut his first solo album, *Ready to Die,* on Bad Boy Records in 1994. He rapped in a deep baritone about the usual gangsta subjects and, unexpectedly, real love and family responsibilities. The album sold nearly 2 million copies.

Although basking in early success, B.I.G. was wary of his celebrity. He carried guns and spoke often of his vulnerability, worried that he could be killed at any time. "I'm scared to death. Scared of getting my brains blown out."

In 1995, *Billboard* selected the Notorious B.I.G. as rap artist of the year. "One More Chance/Stay with Me" from *Ready to Die* was voted best rap single of the year. He also produced albums for others, including Junior M.A.F.I.A, featuring his girlfriend, Lil' Kim, and appeared on Michael Jackson's album *HIStory, Volume 1.*

The world of gangsta rap bristled with bicoastal hostilities. After West Coast rappers Tupac Shakur and Ice T had established a hip-hop style for Death Row Records, Shakur accused B.I.G. of ripping off his sound. They battled in their lyrics, hurling expletives and threats that heightened tensions between rival factions. When Shakur was robbed in New York following a recording session in 1994, he blamed the Notorious B.I.G. for the attack. B.I.G. denied any involvement, and the police found no evidence to connect him to the crime, but the incident brought hostilities to a boiling point.

In September 1996, Tupac Shakur was shot while sitting in his car in Las Vegas after attending a boxing match featuring Mike Tyson. He died six days later. The West Coast gangsta groups blamed B.I.G., who had been miles away. The police never found the killers.

Six months later, in Los Angeles, Biggie himself was gunned down while sitting in his GMC Suburban after leaving a music industry party at the Petersen Automotive Museum on Wilshire Boulevard. As with the Shakur shooting, a nondescript car rolled up next to the Suburban just before a fusillade of bullets struck their target. Despite the presence of several eyewitnesses, the police arrested no one. An ambulance rushed the Notorious B.I.G. to Cedars-Sinai Medical Center, where he died forty-five minutes later. After the Los Angeles County Coroner's Office performed an autopsy, his body was flown to New York.

Lyrics prophesying death, even the singer's own, are characteristic of gangsta rap. Nevertheless, the portentous title of B.I.G.'s first album, *Ready to Die,* and of his posthumously released double CD, *Life After Death . . . 'Til Death Do Us Part,* left fans wondering if he had seen the end coming all along.

BEST KNOWN FOR: His gangsta-suave, death-obsessed persona
FIRST JOB: Drug dealer
AVOCATION: Fostering new musical talent

RITES OF PASSAGE

Fans who raced to Cedars-Sinai hoping to hear good news about the rapper were soon given the grim news of his death. B.I.G.'s wife, Faith Evans, went to the hospital to identify the body, and was joined later that Sunday by B.I.G.'s mother, Voletta Wallace, who flew in from New York.

PAYING RESPECTS

The rapper's fans left flowers, notes, and liquor bottles outside his boyhood home, on St. James Place in the Fort Greene section of Brooklyn. The temporary shrine symbolized the neighborhood's feelings about its most successful citizen. In his way, he had represented hope.

THE FUNERAL

THE SERVICE On Tuesday, March 18, 1997, Christopher Wallace was laid out in an oversized casket at the Frank E. Campbell Funeral Chapel on Madison Avenue in New York. The coffin, made from African mahogany and lined with white velvet, reportedly cost $15,000. Dressed in a white double-breasted suit, a cream-colored shirt, a blue gray tie, and sporting a white "playa" hat, the rap star held his final audience among three hundred fifty invited guests at the chapel.

Hip-hop's superstars paid their respects: Queen Latifah, Flavor Flav of Public Enemy, Lil' Kim, members of the Fugees, Sister Souljah, DMC of Run-DMC, Pepa of Salt-N-Pepa, Mary J. Blige, Junior M.A.F.I.A., and Arista Records head Clive Davis. Former New York City mayor David Dinkins attended at the request of both Combs and Biggie's mother.

B.I.G.'s widow, Faith Evans, sang a gospel song; his mother read from the Bible; and Sean "Puffy" Combs delivered the eulogy. The funeral program featured a quote from B.I.G. spoken the day before his slaying: "I want to wake up with my kids. Get 'em ready for school and take 'em to school. I want to participate in all that. I want to see my kids get old." The service ended with an instrumental recording of the Notorious B.I.G.'s single, "Miss U."

THE PROCESSION Led by a black hearse carrying B.I.G.'s body, a cortege of thirty cars crossed the East River to Brooklyn for the rap star's final visit to his hometown, where mourners had been waiting for hours. People of all ages, from grandparents to grandchildren, lined Fulton Street. Families sat on stoops or peered out of windows to honor the murdered rapper. One hand-lettered sign read, WE LOVE YOU BIGGIE, SAVE OUR YOUTH, STOP THE VIOLENCE.

During the ten-minute procession from Fort Greene to Bedford-Stuyvesant, a scuffle broke out around the corner from Wallace's childhood home, when police used pepper spray and nightsticks to stop exuberant fans from dancing on parked cars. Ten people were arrested, including a reporter from the *New York Times*.

FINAL RESTING PLACE The Notorious B.I.G. was cremated and his remains were divided. Half were given to his wife, Faith Evans, and half sit in a mahogany box in Lil' Kim's living room. Lil' Kim, who moved into B.I.G.'s Teaneck condominium with his mother, says she begins her day by kissing B.I.G.'s urn for daily strength.

NEWS OF THE DAY
MARCH 10, 1997
CAMPAIGN FINANCE COMPLICATES CHINA POLICY

TELEVISION AUDIENCE SHRINKS. OR DOES IT?

OLD FRIENDS, ONCE FELONS, REGROUP TO FIGHT CRIME

BEYOND THE GRAVE
The week before he died, the Notorious B.I.G. was showing off a new tattoo, which bore the following scripture from Psalms:

> "The Lord is my light and my salvation, whom shall I fear?
> The Lord is the truth of my life, of whom shall I be afraid?"

Tracks on *Ready to Die* include "Gimme the Loot," "Machine Gun Funk," "Warning," "Ready to Die," "One More Chance," "#!*@ Me," "Everyday Struggle," "Me & My Bitch," "Respect," and "Suicidal Thoughts."

Tracks on the posthumous *Life After Death . . .'Til Death Do Us Part* include "Somebody's Gotta Die," "Last Day," "I Love the Dough," "What's Beef," "Mo Money Problems . . . More Problems," "Niggas Bleed," "I Got a Story to Tell," "Notorious Thugs," "Sky's the Limit," "My Downfall," and "You're Nobody ('Til Somebody Kill U)."

BY THE NUMBERS
In June 1997, Faith Evans released her tribute to B.I.G., "I'll Be Missing You," produced by Sean "Puffy" Combs, which sold more than three hundred thousand copies to hit number one on the *Billboard* magazine "Hot 100 Singles" chart.

EVA PERÓN

"Evita"

May 7, 1919–July 26, 1952

"Before they put me to sleep, if I do not awake—Viva Perón!" (said just before surgery)

EVITA, WITH EMBALMER, IN FINAL REPOSE.

VITAL STATISTICS

AGE AT DEATH: 33

CAUSE OF DEATH: Uterine cancer

SURVIVORS: Her husband, Argentine president Juan Domingo Perón; her mother, Juana Ibarguren; a brother, Juan Duarte; and three sisters, Blanca, Erminda, and Elisa

HER LIFE

Born into illegitimacy, María Eva Duarte, the youngest child of five, set her sights early on leaving the Argentine village of Junin, where her widowed mother operated a boarding house. Attractive, dark-haired, and slim, the young girl left for Buenos Aires after only two years of high school.

After working in various odd jobs and landing bit parts on the stage, Evita, as she preferred to be known, eventually found steady work at Radio Belgrano, the government-controlled radio station, in the capital city. First performing in radio plays, she furthered her interest in acting and landed roles in several films. Through her persistence, ambition, and cunning, which later became legendary, Evita's salary rose from $35 to $7,000 per month in just a few years. At a broadcasting party in 1943, the twenty-four-year-old actress, now blonde, met General Juan Perón, a forty-nine-year-old widower and undersecretary of the War Ministry. The couple were soon inseparable.

At twenty-six, Evita became one of the most powerful women of her time when she married Perón in October 1945. With a keen understanding of the real concerns of working Argentines, Evita filled Perón's agenda with labor concerns and populist issues, and her outreach to the country's working poor

was instrumental in helping General Perón win the February 1946 presidential election. She remade her role of First Lady into a highly visible, politically powerful position. Her oratorical style, her theatrical gestures at the podium, and her sense of glamour played well to her audiences, who came out by the tens of thousands to hear her speak.

Evita Perón became an ex officio member of her husband's cabinet, setting up offices in the Ministry of Labor and Social Welfare, from which she disbursed food, medical supplies, shelter, jobs, or money to the needy, often deliberately in the presence of reporters and news cameras.

A year after the election, Evita Perón traveled to Europe for a two-month tour. Her public relations trip was a political and personal success. The Spanish people received Evita with great fanfare, and in Rome she met with Pope Pius XII in a private audience. The French feted Evita, and Cardinal Roncalli, the future Pope John XXIII, accompanied her on a tour of Notre Dame cathedral. After basking in the light of European adoration, she returned to Argentina to a hero's welcome.

Capitalizing on the favorable press, Evita established the Eva Perón Foundation in 1947 in order to fund projects that benefited silent constituencies: children, the elderly, the homeless, and single parents. Funded by contributions from labor unions and other groups who dared not refuse Señora Perón, the foundation worked at a fever pitch, building housing and hospitals.

A tireless executive, the First Lady worked until the early hours of the morning and demanded the same commitment from her staff. In addition to her work at the Ministry of Labor and her foundation, in 1949 she became the president of the Perónist Women's Party, which supported the policies of President Perón. She exercised an extraordinary power over the *descamisados* (shirtless ones), the laborers, and fought to keep the once-dominant military and aristocratic oligarchy from returning to power. Weekly she reminded her loyal supporters of Perón's commitment to their needs in her newspaper column "Eva Perón Says."

In 1950, doctors diagnosed Evita with uterine cancer, a fact they kept from her and the public. She declined surgery for abdominal pain, claiming her work schedule prohibited it. The following year Juan Perón and his wife made a bid to run together for president and vice-president. But four days after a rally in support of her nomination, attended by a million supporters, Evita turned down the nomination in an emotional radio address, saying, "I am renouncing the honor, but not the fight." Many believe that she withdrew not because of her illness, but because she feared the military would not support a female candidate.

She campaigned untiringly for her husband and voted for him, in the first vote after Argentine women were granted suffrage, from a hospital bed after finally undergoing surgery. In May 1952, weighing only seventy-seven pounds, she delivered her last speech, attacking her husband's foes while upholding the ideals of Peronism. Frail and emaciated from cancer, Argentina's First Lady insisted on attending her husband's inauguration in June, but it was to be her last public appearance.

Secluded inside the presidential palace with her husband, mother, and sister by her side, Evita Perón died at 8:25 P.M. on Saturday, July 26, 1952.

BEST KNOWN FOR: Her driving ambition and tireless compassion
FIRST JOB: Actress in a stage comedy, *La Señora de los Perez*
AVOCATION: Charity

RITES OF PASSAGE

Upon learning of Evita's illness, many Argentines immediately began praying for her recovery. When the news of her death was confirmed, their outpouring of grief was unprecedented. Evita was more than a symbol of hope; she had become a deity.

THE PREPARATION On Sunday, July 27, Evita's body was transferred to the auditorium of the Ministry of Labor, where she had worked for so many years. In the morning, the immediate family attended a private mass conducted by Father Herman Benitez, Evita's spiritual adviser. Her body was encased in a white mahogany casket with a glass cover. White orchids cascaded down the bier, which had been placed in the flower-filled second-floor auditorium that served as a makeshift chapel.

PAYING RESPECTS

Argentine flags, draped in black, flew at half-staff. Buildings and lampposts in Buenos Aires were similarly shrouded in black bunting. The government declared a thirty-day period of mourning, and its ministers were required to wear black ties or armbands. Those who did not were arrested.

Out of respect for their leader, the General Confederation of Labor (GCL) called for a work stoppage for two days, later adding a third day. The country literally came to a standstill. Ships could not be unloaded, food went undelivered, taxi services halted, and restaurants and shops closed.

Argentine athletes competing in the Olympic Summer Games in Helsinki wore black armbands to their meets. One of them, Reinaldo Corno, said, "the death of the Señora was a terrible handicap for me and all Argentine athletes." The government forbade radio stations from playing anything but religious music or news of Evita's funeral from the time of her death until July 31,

HOMENAJE A EVA PERON

BEREAVED SUPPORTERS GATHER BENEATH A PORTRAIT OF THEIR FIRST LADY IN THE TWO WEEKS OF MOURNING BEFORE HER BURIAL.

HUNDREDS OF THOUSANDS OF ARGENTINES LINE AVENIDA
DE MAYO FOR **EVITA**'S FUNERAL PROCESSION.

five days later. At that time, stations were permitted to feature classical music and news of Perón's lying in state. A ban on dance music was enforced until August 26, one month after her death. The post office began printing Evita's likeness on stamps of all denominations, mandating that, for one year, only stamps bearing her likeness could be used in Argentina.

While President Perón prayed at his wife's bier, Evita's devoted followers rushed the Ministry of Labor building the Sunday morning after her death, overcoming a police barricade, only to be stopped at the doors by guards. Eventually the mourners, who had waited in lines four abreast for ten blocks, were admitted to pay their respects.

The government had announced two days of lying in state with a funeral on the third day, but it responded to the massive outpouring of grief by leaving Evita's body on view for thirteen days. Hundreds of thousands of Argentines traveled to Buenos Aires to have the privilege of glimpsing *la dama de la esperanza* (the lady of hope). Each day, mourners stood for more than ten hours, at times in the winter rain, to say good-bye to their idol.

Floral supplies in Buenos Aires were quickly depleted, and planeloads of fresh flowers arrived daily to meet the demand for memorial wreaths. So numerous were the bouquets placed in front of the Ministry of Labor that the mountain of flowers rose to the second floor, where Evita lay.

On the second day of public viewing, Monday, July 28, the throng of mourners became hysterical and at least four people, possibly as many as eight, were trampled to death. Two thousand mourners were injured. Grieving citizens held torchlight demonstrations in the main squares of Buenos Aires each evening commencing at 8:25 P.M., the hour of Evita's death.

On July 29, hoping that workers would be dissuaded from hanging around the capital city in anticipation of the First Lady's imminent funeral, the government announced an indefinite postponement of the ceremony. Already crippled by work shutdowns, the country needed its people to return to their jobs, yet thousands continued to pour into the city to pay respects.

THE FUNERAL

After more than a fortnight of lying in state, Evita Perón received funeral honors befitting a president who had died in office. The ceremony spanned two days.

THE PROCESSION At 10:15 A.M. on Sunday, August 9, pallbearers placed Eva Perón's coffin on a gun carriage to travel the fifteen-block route to the National Congress Building.

Accompanied by Chopin's "Funeral March," the cortege departed the Ministry of Labor building along the Avenida de Mayo, site of many of Evita's grandest rallies. The gun carriage was pulled by three rows of workers, men and women of the GCL and Perónist Women's Party, wearing black pants and white shirts. Set atop the carriage and wrapped in an Argentine flag was Evita's small, silver-adorned, cedar coffin. Military troops lined the route two deep and presented arms as the cortege passed. Walking behind the carriage, President Perón led the chief mourning party of cabinet ministers and dignitaries. Nurses from the Eva Perón Foundation, union workers, and students flanked the elected officials. Hundreds of thousands stood along the one-mile route.

Evita's body lay in state at the Congress building for twenty-four hours. Again, crowds gathered to view her body. At the request of the Argentine government, Twentieth Century Fox sent a Technicolor film crew to record the two-day event.

On Monday, August 10, seven speakers eulogized Eva Perón at the Congress building before her coffin was transferred to the majestic General Confederation of Labor building, where a lecture hall would serve as a temporary mausoleum. Interior Minister Angel Borlenghi referred to the First Lady as both a "saint" and a "good fairy."

More than 2 million mourners lined the streets to say their farewell. Along the Avenida de Mayo, windows were filled with onlookers who threw flowers onto the passing coffin. A funeral float depicting a giant pair of open hands, symbolizing Evita's generosity, bore her words, "Where there is a worker, there lies the nation." Others carried lit torches representing the eternal flame that would burn in her memory at the Eva Perón Foundation building. Workers threw flower petals in front of one float that carried the message "The flame of your memory will forever live in our hearts."

Despite the previous order in the streets, tragedy struck again on this final day of public grief, when twelve people were killed in the crush and another four thousand were injured.

FINAL RESTING PLACE Evita's death may have provided rest for her soul, but it did not give rest to her body, which traveled nearly as much in death as she had in life. Soon after President Juan Perón was removed from office in 1955, the body of Evita Perón, which had been worked on by a Spanish embalmer for more than a year in anticipation of its permanent display, disappeared from the GCL, where it had remained on view since 1952. Numerous accounts of its whereabouts in the sixteen years before it was unearthed have surfaced. Apparently afraid that her tomb would become a shrine to Perónism, the military stole Evita's remains. During the late 1950s, her body was reportedly stashed in various places in Buenos Aires, including in an attic, in a truck, and on a military base.

The mystery of the whereabouts of Evita's remains ended in 1971 when a note in the will of a former Argentine leader indicated that she was buried in a cemetery in Milan, Italy. Sometime in the late 1950s, Evita's coffin had been shipped there and, possibly with the knowledge of the Vatican, interred in a consecrated grave under a different name.

Once its location was discovered, the exhumed body of Evita Perón was moved to Spain from Italy in a simple black coffin where the exiled Juan Perón and his third wife, Isabel, took possession of it in September 1971. Some reports claim that the body was still perfectly preserved, while others state that it had been "mutilated." When Juan Perón returned to Argentina in 1973 and assumed the presidency again, he left Evita's body in Madrid. After his death a year later, Evita's body was returned to Buenos Aires. Hoping to secure her eternal rest twenty-four years after her death, Evita's family buried her in 1976 in the Duarte family crypt under triple steel plates.

When Evita withdrew her bid for vice president in 1951 in a radio announcement, she may as well have written her own epitaph: "There was a woman alongside General Perón who took to him the hopes and needs of the people to satisfy them, and her name was Evita."

NEWS OF THE DAY
JULY 26, 1952
FAROUK OUT;
QUITS EGYPT AFTER COUP

EVA PERÓN DIES IN ARGENTINA;
A POWER AS PRESIDENT'S WIFE

OTHER DEATHS

On July 28, General Juan Vacca, the former undersecretary of the army and a compatriot of President Perón, died from injuries sustained when he was trampled in the crush to view Evita's body.

AROUND THE WORLD

An editorial in the *New York Times* commemorating her death called Evita "the most remarkable woman in Latin American chronicles . . . In death as in life, Eva Perón remains a power in her land."

BEYOND THE GRAVE

Evita Perón's autobiography, *The Purpose of My Life,* published in 1951, sold more copies in Argentina than any other Spanish-language book in print. Schools adopted it as compulsory reading. In 1996 the book was reissued in English entitled *In My Own Words,* including a previously unpublished deathbed tirade against the church and the military, "My Message."

LAST WISHES

Eva Perón had requested that she be buried temporarily in the GCL's building in the Buenos Aires dock district and moved to a memorial that she had designed from her deathbed. The memorial was never built.

MEMORIALS AND TRIBUTES

The Union of Food Industry Workers cabled Pope Pius XII on August 1, 1952, to request that the process of beatification of Eva Perón begin immediately. In Argentina, especially among union workers and the poor, Perón was often referred to as "Saint Evita." More than forty thousand workers wrote to the pope supporting canonization.

On August 8, 1952, the legislature of the province of Buenos Aires voted to change its capital's name from La Plata to Eva Perón.

In 1978, Andrew Lloyd Webber and Tim Rice's musical *Evita* premiered in London. The Tony Award–winning musical featured the hit song, "Don't Cry for Me Argentina," and won critical praise.

THE HEREAFTER

In 1955, just a few months after an annual tribute to his deceased wife, President Juan D. Perón was ousted by the Argentine military in the Liberating Revolution. Without Evita by his side, Perón lost power and fled the country, eventually settling in Spain. Under the new government, owning a picture of Evita Perón was a crime punishable by years of imprisonment. Perón returned to power in October 1973 as president with his third wife, Isabel de Perón, in the vice-presidential position that had eluded Evita. He died in office on July 1, 1974, and was succeeded by his wife, who became the first female president in the Western Hemisphere.

EDITH PIAF

"Little Sparrow"

December 19, 1915–October 11, 1963

"Non, je ne regrette rien." ("No, I don't regret a thing.")

∾ A TYPICALLY TRAGIC **PIAF** ALBUM COVER

VITAL STATISTICS

AGE AT DEATH: 47

CAUSE OF DEATH: Internal hemorrhaging caused by a liver ailment

SURVIVORS: Her husband, Theo Sarapo

CLOSE CALLS: On three occasions between 1958–1959, Piaf was seriously injured in car accidents. A passenger each time, she was hospitalized with head injuries, broken ribs, and various cuts and bruises. And in February 1959 she collapsed while performing in New York and endured four-hour emergency surgery for a perforated stomach and internal hemorrhaging.

HER LIFE

France's most celebrated chanteuse was born Edith Gassion to a cabaret-singing, gypsy mother and an acrobat father. Left with her grandmother, who lived in squalor, she was later raised by a member of her aunt's family who worked in a brothel. Traveling occasionally with her adoring, itinerant father, she showed no interest in acrobatics, but she did display a talent for singing. After moving to Paris with her father, his mistress, and their baby, teenage Edith earned money singing on the streets. She fell in love and bore an illegitimate daughter, Marcelle, who died of meningitis in childhood. By this time Edith had fallen in love with another man and was singing in small clubs frequented by the demimonde of French society.

In 1935, cabaret owner Louis Leplée "discovered" the young singer and helped shape her image, fitting her in a simple black dress, selecting ten songs from her repertoire of love ballads, and putting her onstage at his chic dinner club in a neighborhood of the Avenue Champs-Elysées. The French entertainer Maurice Chevalier said of her debut, "She's got what it takes." Leplée christened the four-foot, ten-inch waif, "Piaf," French slang for "sparrow," a name reflecting her small stature and her style of warbling.

Piaf's next paramour, Raymond Asso, transformed her into a star, teaching her vocal technique and social etiquette. Before World War II, Piaf performed on the radio and enjoyed her first hit record, *Mon Legionnaire,* becoming a sensation in Paris, where she performed at packed music halls. During the war years, despite her popularity and requests for her to perform, Piaf sang only for audiences made up of prisoners of war. Captive in the city during Paris's wartime occupation, Piaf collaborated with artist Jean Cocteau on a play written for her, *Le Bel Indifferent* (1940), and appeared in her first film, *Montmartre-sur-Seine,* in 1941.

Edith Piaf's intense, tragic style of singing became her signature. The petite chanteuse filled auditoriums with her strong voice, which trembled with lovesickness, vibrated with agony, and trilled with joy. Her songs, many of which she wrote or cowrote, centered on themes of spurned love, unrequited love, or tragic love. Onstage, Piaf's emotional performances brought audiences to tears. Although she sang primarily in French, Piaf became an international star, known best in North America for her hit song, "La Vie En Rose."

The tragedy Piaf had known as a youth became a recurring theme in her art and her life. After the war, she fell in love with boxer Marcel Cerdan, only to lose him in an airplane crash two years later. She married a singer in 1952 and divorced him in 1957. In between she had a host of lovers, but happiness eluded her.

In spite of the hardships of her childhood, Piaf was known as a generous woman. She amassed a fortune from her singing engagements around the world, but she spent most of her money supporting friends and family. Piaf encouraged young talent and helped launch the careers of two of her discoveries, singer Charles Aznavour and singer-actor Yves Montand, who also became her lover.

Sickness plagued Piaf from childhood, when she had experienced temporary blindness as a result of a virus. As an adult, her alcohol and drug use contributed to her weakened state. Her performances required such energy that they often left her depleted and bedridden for weeks. Arthritis wracked her body, yet the "little sparrow" continued to go onstage, claiming that singing was her life. Critics pointed to Piaf's suffering as the source of her artistry.

Piaf married for a final time in 1962, to a young singer, Theo Sarapo, twenty years her junior, whose career she promoted generously. That same year, while in visible pain, she gave a performance at the Olympia Music Hall in Paris. The recording of that concert sold more than a million copies in France alone.

Illness forced Piaf to cancel an October 3, 1963, performance in New York City at the Mark Hellinger Theater. Suffering from a liver ailment, the singer retreated to her home in the south of France. Wishing to die in Paris, she hired an ambulance to drive the five hundred miles to her apartment there. On October 11, 1963, with her husband by her side, the "little sparrow" died of an internal hemorrhage before reaching her destination.

BEST KNOWN FOR: Her emotive voice
FIRST JOB: Varnishing wooden soles of shoes
AVOCATION: Mentoring younger singers

RITES OF PASSAGE
PAYING RESPECTS
Visitors to Piaf's Paris apartment on the day she died included Yves Montand and Charles Aznavour. Visibly shaken, they paid their final respects as she lay on her bed with a rose in one hand and an orchid in the other. Government-owned French radio canceled its scheduled programming to play a tribute to Edith Piaf and her music.

Piaf's fans were as devoted to their star in her death as they had been in her life. On Sunday, October 13, more than one hundred thousand mourners waited outside Edith Piaf's home near the Bois de Boulogne for a chance to view her body. The crowd, mostly women, overtook the neighborhood and police were forced to redirect traffic. Shoes were lost and fans were knocked to the ground in the crush.

THE FUNERAL
THE PROCESSION On Monday, October 14, a mob of Piaf fans again waited outside the singer's home as a flower-laden hearse and three-car cortege embarked for the cemetery across town. Along the route, admirers observed a respectful silence as the forty-seven-year-old chanteuse was taken to her final resting place.

THE SERVICE Since Edith Piaf had divorced and remarried into the Greek Orthodox Church, the Roman Catholic Church prevented her from receiving a Catholic funeral mass. The only funeral service was performed at her graveside where a chaplain from the Catholic Union of the Theater and Music Hall delivered prayers and a blessing over her coffin before its burial.

FINAL RESTING PLACE Having long since left Belleville, the working-class neighborhood of her childhood, Edith Piaf was put to rest at Père Lachaise Cemetery, coincidentally situated adjacent to it.

Outside Paris's most distinguished resting place, an excitable crowd of forty thousand fans awaited the arrival of Piaf's hearse. When it approached, police were unable to contain the surging mob. People fainted, fell, and were trampled as the crowd tried to reach the singer's tomb. In a scene more appropriate to a music-hall farce, mourners hurdled over tombstones, running over centuries-old graves for a glimpse of the chanteuse's coffin. In the cramped space around Piaf's open grave, Aznavour, Montand, and actress Marlene Dietrich rubbed shoulders with working-class fans. One man even fell into Piaf's open grave.

Although not a state funeral, Piaf's send-off had all the flair of one, with multitudes of loyal fans and her fellow entertainers, including Tino Rossi and Gilbert Becauds, in attendance. French notables were torn between attending the popular singer's funeral or the tribute to Jean Cocteau, who had died the same day as Piaf. Dietrich managed both, rushing from Père Lachaise to Milly-la-Forêt, a town just south of Paris, where Cocteau lay in state.

NEWS OF THE DAY
OCTOBER 12, 1963
U.S. EXCHANGES 2 RUSSIAN SPIES FOR 2 AMERICANS

ALGERIANS SEIZE 3 REBEL TOWNS

JEAN COCTEAU AND EDITH PIAF ARE DEAD IN FRANCE

OTHER DEATHS
Artist Jean Cocteau died of a stroke at age seventy-four in Paris, just seven hours after Edith Piaf expired. In addition to his 1941 stage play written for Piaf, he had also written the preface to her 1958 autobiography, *Au Bal de la Chance* (Wheel of Fortune). Upon hearing the news of his friend's death, he remarked, "I had a fever since this morning, and I must say that the death of Edith Piaf has caused renewed sadness and discomfort." A few hours later, Cocteau said, "The boat is going down." These were his last words.

BEYOND THE GRAVE
ODD COINCIDENCES
Piaf's last performance was at Paris's Bobino Théâtre, the same Left Bank music hall that later hosted Josephine Baker's final stage appearance in 1975.

MEMORIALS AND TRIBUTES
Piaf's home on rue Crespin du Gast in Paris is now a private museum dedicated to the life and music of the star. On display are the singer's photographs, jewelry, furniture, and other memorabilia.

≈ **PIAF**'S HEARSE, SURROUNDED BY THOUSANDS OF MOURNERS, SLOWLY MAKES ITS WAY TO PÈRE LACHAISE CEMETERY, OCTOBER 14, 1963.

POPE JOHN XXIII

"The Pope of Goodness"

November 25, 1881–June 3, 1963

*"It often happens that I wake up at night and begin to think about a serious problem and decide
I must tell the pope about it. Then I wake up completely and remember that I am the pope."*

THE POPE'S BODY, AS CARRIED BY
BEARERS THROUGH ST. PETER'S SQUARE.

VITAL STATISTICS

AGE AT DEATH: 81

CAUSE OF DEATH: Peritonitis resulting from a stomach tumor

SURVIVORS: A sister, Assunta; three brothers, Zaverio, Giuseppe, and Alfredo; and eighteen nephews and nieces

LAST WORDS: "Ut unum sint." ("That they may be one.") Jesus Christ is said to have spoken these words after the Last Supper.

HIS LIFE

One of thirteen children born to a farming family near Bergamo, Italy, Angelo Giuseppe Roncalli worked as a farmer before entering the Roman Catholic priesthood in 1904. He served in World War I, first as a sergeant in the medical corps and then as a lieutenant in the chaplain corps. After the war, he worked in Rome for the Congregation of the Propagation of the Faith. In 1925, Pope Pius XI assigned him to Bulgaria as an apostolic visitor, making him an archbishop.

Ten years later, the pope sent Archbishop Roncalli as his apostolic delegate to Greece and Turkey, where he remained during World War II. In Istanbul, the archbishop served in a diplomatic role as a liaison between the two feuding nations and forged a friendship with the Eastern factions of the church that had long been estranged from Rome.

His success in Turkey prepared him for an equally demanding position as nuncio to France. Reeling from the divisiveness engendered by World War II, French Catholics needed a sensitive leader to manage the passions between Gaullists and Vichyites. During this period, Roncalli also served as the Vatican observer for UNESCO. In 1953, Pope Pius XII made the seventy-two-year-old Roncalli a cardinal. A short time later Roncalli was named Patriarch of Venice, a position he assumed with vigor.

On October 28, 1958, after Pope Pius XII died, Roncalli's fellow cardinals elected him as their next pope despite grave concerns about his advanced age. He took the name Pope John XXIII. The new pope surprised his colleagues with ambitious plans for his papacy, calling for a general ecumenical council, known as the Second Vatican Council or Vatican II, to address religious and secular issues facing the Roman Catholic Church. The Second Vatican Council convened on October 11, 1962, and resulted in modernizing changes such as using vernacular language instead of Latin in the liturgy.

Known as "the people's pope," John XXIII proved to be inspired and energetic in his four-and-a-half-year papacy. His 1963 encyclical, *Pacem in Terris* (Peace in the World), was considered an important social discourse on achieving peace through freedom and justice in the international community. It joined his 1961 encyclical, *Mater et Magistra* (Christianity and Social Progress), on social reforms and economic problems in the world, to form a treatise on the Catholic Church's willingness to work with others in a commitment to securing global peace and prosperity. During his papacy, Pope John XXIII reached out to communist governments, tried to mend the differences between Eastern and Western factions of the church, and created the Secretariat for Promoting Christian Unity.

Suffering from abdominal pain, Pope John XXIII knew he was gravely ill by the time the Second Vatican Council convened. Doctors discovered a stomach tumor the next month, yet the pope still managed to preside over the proceedings during the council's first year. His successor, Pope Paul VI, saw Vatican II through to completion.

Pope John XXIII received an enormous, worldwide outpouring of sympathy when his condition became public. The Vatican issued frequent bulletins on the pontiff's declining health and tens of thousands of people prayed for His Holiness during a four-day vigil outside the Vatican.

On Monday, June 3, 1963, in the papal chamber, Pope John XXIII died in the presence of his family, his physicians, his confessor, two personal attendants, a nurse, and Amleto Cicognani, Vatican Secretariat of State. The pope received the sacrament of extreme unction thirty minutes prior to dying. When Cardinal Cicognani announced in Latin, "Vere Papa mortuus est" ("In truth the pope is dead"), those present fell to their knees and prayed, before arising to approach the pope's bed and kiss his right hand. The papal chamber was sealed with locks and chains and protected by two armored guards with swords drawn, as is customary when the Vatican is without a pope. That evening, thirty-five thousand people attended a mass for the pope on the steps of St. Peter's Basilica. The service concluded just as Vatican radio broadcast news of the pope's death. The bronze doors to Vatican City that face St. Peter's Square were then closed, a custom indicating that the pope has died.

BEST KNOWN FOR: His humanitarianism and efforts to promote peace and interfaith understanding
FIRST JOB: Farmer
AVOCATION: Peacemaking

RITES OF PASSAGE
THE PREPARATION
By order of Cardinal Masella, the chief executive of the Vatican, the pontiff was moved from his rooms in the Apostolic Palace, where he had died, to his private apartment in the Vatican Palace late Monday evening. There, on the morning of Tuesday, June 4, foreign dignitaries paid their respects on behalf of their governments. Because the United States did not yet have diplomatic relations with the Vatican, it was not represented.

PAYING RESPECTS
The Italian government closed schools and courts on Tuesday, June 4, and ordered the flag to fly at half-staff for three days. Mourning posters featuring black-bordered portraits of the pope appeared all over Rome.

THE FUNERAL
THE PROCESSION Later on Tuesday afternoon, the bells of St. Peter's tolled, announcing the papal procession. Led by palatine and Swiss guards, the procession departed through the bronze Vatican doors and entered St. Peter's Square. The procession included officers of the Papal Gendarmes, the Noble Guard, and Swiss Guard, who accompanied the body of Pope John XXIII to the basilica. Two acolytes followed carrying a spearheaded cross.

The cortege included torch-bearing grooms, a reference to an era when popes rode white mules, followed by the Julian Choir and a cadre of student priests. The pope's body was openly displayed on a litter carried by eight bearers who were usually responsible for carrying the pope on a portable throne. Chamberlains of the Cape and Sword in Elizabethan costume and distinguished Vatican ministers responsible for the pope's household preceded the litter.

Pope John XXIII's three brothers, sister, three nephews, and two nieces (both nuns) followed the bier. Behind them walked the pontifical court, comprising thirty cardinals wearing mourning robes of violet.

Inside St. Peter's Basilica, Christendom's largest church, Pope John XXIII lay on a fifteen-foot-high catafalque under Michelangelo's dome and before the Altar of the Confession, surrounded by burning candles. Elegantly adorned in brocade and velvet pontifical cloaks with a gold miter on his head, the pontiff wore red velvet slippers embroidered with gold crosses, and his red-gloved hands held a crucifix and rosary.

Beginning at 8:00 A.M. on Wednesday, June 5, mourners waited in lines more than a mile long to pay their respects to the man who would be known posthumously as "the Pope of Goodness." His Holiness lay in state until 5:00 P.M. on Thursday, June 6. More than one hundred fifty thousand mourners had come to St. Peter's to pray.

THE SERVICE One hour after public viewing ended, the private burial service for the pontiff commenced. In addition to cardinals, bishops, archbishops, and patriarchs, nine Roncalli family members and fifty members of the diplomatic corps witnessed the solemn ritual of burial. Cardinal Ritter of St. Louis, Cardinal Meyer of Chicago, and Cardinal McIntyre of Los Angeles represented the Catholic Church in the United States.

St. Peter's was draped in black, and invitees not dressed in clerical garments or uniforms wore evening dress as a sign of mourning. The pope rested on a catafalque in an apse between the Altar of Confession and the Altar of the Chair, where the services were conducted. A triple coffin weighing more than one thousand pounds was waiting nearby. Lined in red satin, the first casket was made of cypress wood; it had been placed inside a lead coffin with a bronze lid, which in turn rested within the third coffin, made of mahogany.

Monsignor Pericle Felici performed the funeral ceremonies. The clergy of Rome wore surplices and the crimson-clad canons of St. Peter's bore lit torches. One hundred voices of the Julian Choir sang "Miserere" ("Have mercy"), the first word of the Fiftieth Psalm.

After Monsignor Nicola Metta read the "act of burial" in Latin, four attendants lifted the litter bearing Pope John XXIII and placed him into his coffin. Another priest, Monsignor Amleto Tondini, delivered the eulogy, inserting a parchment copy of the eulogy in a metal tube and placing it in the pope's innermost coffin. Two velvet sacks of coins and medals, representative of the coinage struck during the pope's four-year reign, were also placed inside the casket.

The cardinals each made their farewells to His Holiness, after which silk cloths were draped over the pope's face and hands. The pontiff's entire body was then covered with a crimson silk sheet. A brocade blanket cloaked the open coffin and attendants pushed the coffin on a wheeled cart to the entrance of the burial crypt, underneath St. Peter's main altar.

Only a handful of people witnessed the closing of Pope John XXIII's coffin and its transfer to the stone sarcophagus in a small, whitewashed chapel, facing the tombs of His Holiness's predecessors Pope Pius XI and Pope Pius XII. A small wreath of carnations and lilies came from inmates at Regina Coeli prison in Rome, where prisoners fondly remembered the pope's visit, one his first official acts as pontiff. Although the crypt was off-limits to visitors, the public came to pray at the wooden barriers nearby.

The burial of Pope John XXIII began a nine-day period of mourning (not including the Feast of the Trinity on June 9 and the Feast of Corpus Christi on June 13), and each day at St. Peter's a requiem mass was held for the repose of the pope's soul. The final mass, on Monday, June 17, completed the official funeral ceremonies for the 261st pope, who was given the five-fold blessing and absolution reserved for bishops and pontiffs. Since the pope's mortal remains now resided underneath the altar in a crypt, his body was represented by a three-tiered catafalque. Rising twenty-five feet above the basilica's floor, the nineteenth-century wooden platform was topped by a red velvet cushion carrying the papal crown, the triregnum. Ninety-six candles burned in silver holders surrounding the catafalque. Seventy-five of the eighty-two cardinals attended the mass, as did representatives of Europe's royal families. Eighty-four delegations including the United States' four-member group, headed by Vice President Lyndon B. Johnson, were present. Mayor Robert Wagner of New York City also sent two representatives to the funeral. The seventy-third Lombardy Regiment, to which the Pope had been attached during World War I, presented military honors outside the basilica as the mass was celebrated.

Two days after Pope John XXIII's mourning ended, the Sacred College of Cardinals went into seclusion in the Vatican to elect his successor. Cardinal Montini of Milan was elected on June 22, 1963, taking the name of Pope Paul VI.

FINAL RESTING PLACE Although Pope John XXIII had requested that he be buried not as the Supreme Pontiff in St. Peter's but more simply as the Bishop of Rome, in the Church of St. John Lateran, the Vatican felt his tomb should remain in a place of honor at St. Peter's.

NEWS OF THE DAY
JUNE 4, 1963
POPE JOHN XXIII IS DEAD AT 81, ENDING 4 1/2-YEAR REIGN DEVOTED TO PEACE AND CHRISTIAN UNITY

JUNE 17, 1963
SOVIET ORBITS WOMAN ASTRONAUT NEAR BYKOVSKY FOR DUAL FLIGHT; THEY TALK BY RADIO ARE PUT ON TV

BEN-GURION STEPS DOWN ISRAELI CABINET SURPRISED

AROUND THE WORLD
Flags in New York City were lowered to half-staff. The United Nations, but not the United States, also lowered its flag out of respect; the State Department issued a statement saying that the United States lowers its flag only for United States citizens.

BEYOND THE GRAVE
Pope John XXIII was the second pontiff named Pope John XXIII. The first was deposed in 1417, during a time when three men simultaneously claimed the title of Supreme Pontiff, and has since been designated an antipope.

MEMORIALS AND TRIBUTES
Efforts to canonize Pope John XXIII began shortly after his death. Thirty-seven years later, on September 3, 2000, the Roman Catholic Church's Jubilee year, Pope John Paul II beatified Pope John XXIII to a cheering crowd of eighty thousand people assembled in St. Peter's Square. Only four other popes had achieved sainthood in the previous nine hundred years.

THE "**POPE OF GOODNESS**," LYING IN STATE
BEFORE THE ALTAR OF CONFESSION IN ST. PETER'S BASILICA
IN ROME

ELVIS PRESLEY

"The King"

January 8, 1935–August 16, 1977

*"Some people tap their feet, some people snap their fingers, and some people sway back and forth.
I just sorta do 'em all together, I guess."*

A POLICEMAN SALUTES AS **THE KING**'S
COFFIN, VISIBLE IN THE BACK OF THE HEARSE,
DEPARTS GRACELAND.

VITAL STATISTICS

AGE AT DEATH: 42

CAUSE OF DEATH: Heart attack caused by cardiac arrhythmia

SURVIVORS: A daughter, Lisa Marie; his father, Vernon
                      Presley; his grandmother, Minnie Mae Presley;
                      and his fiancée, Ginger Alden

LAST WORDS: "I'm going into the bathroom to read."

HIS LIFE

Born into poverty in Tupelo, Mississippi, Elvis was the only surviving child of Gladys and Vernon Presley; his twin brother had been stillborn. Raised by a religious and doting mother, Elvis sang in a church choir and, at the age of ten, won a singing contest at school.

In 1953, Presley paid four dollars to cut a record for his mother at a Memphis studio. At the studio, the proprietor, Sam Phillips, heard something special in Presley's voice, and thought the young singer might be the white crossover blues singer he'd been looking for. In 1954, Phillips recorded five singles with Presley on his Sun Records label, including "That's All Right, Mama" and "Blue Moon of Kentucky." Each new Presley hit got considerable play on local radio, and Presley's career was underway.

When Phillips arranged a tour for Presley and "The Hillbilly Cats," Elvis developed a following due in equal parts to his voice, rhythmic movements, and tight pants. It was the beginning of the Presley phenomenon. RCA Victor capitalized on his regional success and bought Presley's singles from Sun Records for $35,000, putting "Colonel" Tom Parker, a talent manager, in charge of his career and launching the singer to stardom.

Presley's notorious appearance on *The Ed Sullivan Show* in 1956 featured pelvic gyrations so outrageous that the producers only shot the singer from the waist up, earning him the nickname "Elvis the Pelvis." That same year Elvis hit it big with "Heartbreak Hotel," his first song to sell a million copies. Over the next twenty years, he would repeat that feat fifty-four times.

Presley's success hinged on his sultry good looks and boy-next-door charisma, in addition to his singing voice. In 1956, Elvis starred in *Love Me Tender,* the first of his thirty-three films, thinly veiled promotional vehicles that nonetheless appealed to a new generation of rock 'n' roll teenagers.

Between 1958 and 1960, Elvis served first as a private, then as a sergeant in the U.S. Army, stationed in West Germany, where he met his future wife, Priscilla Beaulieu. The couple commenced a seven-year courtship before finally exchanging vows in Las Vegas in 1967.

Presley stopped performing in movies after 1969's *The Trouble with Girls.* He went on to launch a successful nightclub career, taking his show on the road to sold-out arenas around the country. After his 1973 divorce, he became increasingly reclusive, depressed, overweight, and dependent on prescription drugs. He was notoriously nocturnal. On the day of his death, Elvis had played racquetball at his Memphis home, Graceland, with his fiancée, Ginger Alden, and another couple until six in the morning. Shortly thereafter he went to read in the bathroom and had a fatal heart attack.

BEST KNOWN FOR: Transforming the Southern black rhythm and
                      blues sound into rock 'n' roll; his gyrating
                      pelvis

FIRST JOB: Usher in a movie theater

AVOCATION: Collecting cars, especially Cadillacs

RITES OF PASSAGE

THE PREPARATION

Presley was pronounced dead at Baptist Hospital in Memphis on the afternoon of Tuesday, August 16, 1977. After an autopsy, his body was delivered to the Memphis Funeral Home for embalming. At half past ten the next morning, a police escort accompanied Presley's hearse to Graceland.

PAYING RESPECTS

As soon as the news broke that the King was dead, fans converged on Memphis. Booked to capacity, Delta Airlines added more flights, and fans played hooky from work and bolted to Graceland in the hopes of seeing their fallen idol one last time.

The bereaved began to assemble outside the Presley mansion as early as three o'clock in the morning on Wednesday, August 17. The local police and firefighters were joined by Air National Guardsmen to maintain order. Although Graceland had never been open to the public, the Presley family offered fans an opportunity to view the King's body in the foyer of his home on that afternoon between three and five o'clock. Authorities had difficulty keeping zealous fans from scaling the compound's walls and crashing the gates, and police threatened to close Graceland unless the crowd calmed down. A separate area on the lawn was used for a temporary first-aid clinic to treat those suffering from the effects of the ninety-degree heat.

As they quickly discovered, the Presley family had grossly underestimated the demand for the privilege of seeing the King. Viewing was extended until half past six, but of the nearly one hundred thousand fans who had arrived at Graceland that day, only twenty-five thousand made it inside. When the viewing period ended, police barricaded the gates, but the crowds refused to disperse and hundreds kept vigil outside Graceland throughout the night.

Fans everywhere stormed music stores, depleting most of the Presley inventory. Radio stations in Memphis played only tunes associated with the King in tribute to the native son, and they planned a one-minute period of silence for Thursday, August 18, at the hour of the funeral services. That day, governors of both Tennessee and Mississippi ordered that their state flags be flown at half-staff.

THE FUNERAL

THE SERVICE A private funeral was held on Thursday, August 18, at 2:00 P.M., in Graceland's music room, where family and close friends, including actress Ann-Margret and her husband, Roger Smith; actor George Hamilton; musician Chet Atkins; Presley's manager "Colonel" Tom Parker; and Presley's ex-wife, Priscilla Presley, gathered for the two-hour service. Elvis, dressed in a white suit and tie and a blue shirt that his father had given him for Christmas, was laid to rest in a nine-hundred-pound seamless copper casket that had been flown in from Oklahoma City. Family friend and minister of Wooddale Church of Christ, C. W. Bradley, officiated at the funeral service. Musical numbers, including "How Great Thou Art" and "Sweet, Sweet Spirit," were performed by the Stamps Quartet, Presley's gospel back-up group.

After the service, the casket was removed by pallbearers including Joe Esposito, Presley's road manager; Dr. George Nichopoulos, Presley's personal physician; former Memphis disc jockey George Klein; guitarist and Graceland resident Charlie Hodge; friend and music publisher Lamar Fike; cousins Billy Smith and Gene Smith; and friend Jerry Schilling. At approximately four o'clock, a white hearse carrying Presley's remains led the forty-nine-car cortege to the burial site.

FINAL RESTING PLACE Forest Hill Cemetery Midtown closed its gates to the public early Thursday morning to prepare Elvis's crypt, just a short distance from the grave of his mother, for the afternoon burial service.

At the cemetery a second private service was held in the chapel adjacent to the mausoleum, witnessed by 150 mourners. Vernon Presley entered the crypt where his son lay, kissed the rose-covered coffin, and left visibly shaken, supported by family members. When the mourners had departed, the cemetery crew sealed the crypt with two slabs of concrete and one of marble. Finally, at 4:30 P.M., the iron gates of Presley's mausoleum were closed.

Florists in Memphis were besieged with requests from around the world. At the cemetery there were more than thirty-one-hundred arrangements in the shapes of guitars, animals, and messages. On the day following Presley's burial, florists stripped the bouquets and began distributing floral souvenirs to fifty thousand of his fans, many of whom, in their greed, grabbed at bouquets rather than single stems and overran the cemetery, causing chaos.

Presley's entombment did not stop the flow of fans arriving in Memphis. After the interment, traffic was bumper to bumper along the three-and-a-half-mile stretch between Forest Hill and Graceland, which had become a sort of Mecca for distraught fans.

On October 3, 1977, the bodies of Elvis Presley and his mother, Gladys Smith Presley, were removed from their crypt at Forest Hill Cemetery Midtown and transported in two white hearses to Graceland, where they were reinterred on the south side of the mansion's new prayer garden chapel. When Elvis's father died in 1979, he joined his family at Graceland, as did Presley's grandmother the following year.

NEWS OF THE DAY
AUGUST 17, 1977
ELVIS PRESLEY DIES;
ROCK SINGER WAS 42

FORD GIVES SUPPORT TO NEW AGREEMENT ON PANAMA CANAL

BREZHNEV DEPICTS CARTER'S OVERTURE AS A POSITIVE MOVE

OTHER DEATHS
Two young mourners, Alice Marie Hovatar and Juanita Joanne Johnson, were killed and a third was critically injured when a drunk, teenage motorist lost control of his 1963 Ford, driving it into a crowd of three hundred who were holding a vigil outside Graceland on the day that Elvis was buried.

AROUND THE WORLD
Elvis was mourned as deeply in England and France as he was at home. Record sales soared in the days after his death; British fan clubs that had planned to celebrate their twentieth anniversaries instead held memorial services.

BEYOND THE GRAVE
Elvis was buried wearing a ring that had the initials "TCB" emblazoned on a lightning bolt, which he wore often in life. The King prided himself on "taking care of business in a flash."

In 1993, the U.S. Postal Service planned to print a first-class stamp commemorating Elvis Presley, inviting the public to choose between a likeness of Elvis from the 1970s and one from the 1950s. The public responded enthusiastically, and the Elvis Presley stamp carrying his 1950s portrait was printed. It was the single largest printing of an issue in the service's history: 500 million stamps.

ODD COINCIDENCES

Gladys Presley, Elvis's mother, died of a heart attack on August 14, 1958, at forty-two, the same age as her son.

THE HEREAFTER

Graceland was opened to the public in 1982. Elvis Presley Enterprises offers tours to six hundred thousand people a year. The company, through its licensing deals and Graceland receipts, continues to generate enormous revenue for its sole owner and Presley's heir, Lisa Marie Presley.

In 1984, Presley's estate established the Elvis Presley Charitable Trust (EPCT) to support community programs, one of which, Presley Place, is a planned rent-free residential facility for homeless families.

Almost as soon as Elvis died, rumors that he was still alive circulated worldwide. Elvis "sightings" were reported even within twenty-four hours of the King's interment and are still regularly recounted in tabloid magazines.

MOURNERS HOLD **ELVIS** PRAYER SHEETS AT MEMORIAL FOR THE KING.

FRANKLIN D. ROOSEVELT

"FDR"

January 30, 1882– April 12, 1945

"The only thing we have to fear is fear itself."

ROOSEVELT, FISHING IN WARM SPRINGS, GEORGIA, WHERE HE WOULD RETREAT FOR HEALTH REASONS BEFORE HIS DEATH.

VITAL STATISTICS

AGE AT DEATH:	63
CAUSE OF DEATH:	Cerebral hemorrhage
SURVIVORS:	His wife, Eleanor Roosevelt; and five children, Anna Eleanor, James, Elliott, Franklin Delano Jr., and John
LAST WORDS:	"I have a terrific headache."

HIS LIFE

Born to a well-to-do family in Hyde Park, New York, Roosevelt was an only child. His mother, who was twenty-six years younger than his father, doted on her son, hiring foreign-speaking home tutors for him and taking him to Europe during the summer. Roosevelt attended preparatory school at Groton and graduated from Harvard University in 1904. He then attended Columbia University School of Law in New York City and, before graduating, he passed the state examinations qualifying him to practice law.

Franklin Delano Roosevelt's eminent family name and hearty good looks enabled him to enter any profession he liked. Although he had prepared for a law career, he, along with his wife (and distant cousin) Eleanor Roosevelt, became deeply passionate about the plight of underprivileged Americans. This early interest in civil liberties led the young Democrat into the political arena where he was first elected state senator from Dutchess County, New York, in 1910.

Having watched the career of his cousin Teddy Roosevelt, Franklin was a natural at politics. At the 1912 Democratic National Convention, Franklin backed the presidential nomination of Woodrow Wilson, who subsequently appointed him assistant secretary of the Navy. In 1920, Franklin received national attention as the running mate of presidential hopeful Governor James Cox of Ohio (who lost the election to Warren G. Harding).

One year after his vice-presidential bid, Roosevelt contracted poliomyelitis, leaving him a paraplegic at the age of thirty-nine. He spent the next seven years in physical rehabilitation. Encouraged by Eleanor to remain committed to his ideals through politics, Roosevelt attended the 1924 Democratic National Convention, where he unsuccessfully nominated New York governor Alfred Smith as the Democrats' presidential candidate. Four years later, when Smith finally captured the presidential nomination, he convinced Roosevelt to run for governor of New York.

In 1928, Franklin D. Roosevelt was able to surmount his physical handicap and the entrenched Republicanism in upstate counties to win the New York governorship. Exuding charm and compassion, Roosevelt had dispelled concerns about his mobility and stamina with a vigorous campaign. Although Herbert Hoover won the presidential election that year, Roosevelt and his Democratic Party now had a visible platform for their progressive reforms in New York. Buoyed by the popularity of his policies in New York state, as well as the country's disenchantment with Hoover, Franklin Delano Roosevelt was nominated for and won the 1932 presidential election.

When Roosevelt assumed leadership the United States was three years into the Great Depression and suffering the greatest economic hardship in its modern history. Roosevelt responded to this bleak scenario with enterprising social reforms under the banner of the New Deal. Gradually, confidence returned, Americans went back to work, great public works were built, and Social Security was established. Roosevelt forever changed the relationship between the federal government and its citizens, the government becoming their protector, provider, and partner.

He was elected to the office of president four consecutive times, an unprecedented feat never to be repeated by any subsequent president. The dawn of Roosevelt's third term brought his greatest challenge—World War II. While the United States had largely isolated itself from warfare, Roosevelt insisted on helping English prime minister Winston Churchill by supplying surplus weapons and equipment.

After Japan bombed Pearl Harbor, Roosevelt announced in an unforgettable radio address, "Yesterday, December 7, 1941—a date which will live in infamy—the United States of America was suddenly and deliberately attacked by naval and air forces of the Empire of Japan." The United States immediately declared war. Under Roosevelt's leadership as commander in chief, the U.S. citizenry rallied to produce war materials at a rate never seen before, and the U.S. military fought with valor. President Roosevelt kept the light of freedom burning in the hearts and minds of Americans during his "fireside chats" on the radio, which he had conducted regularly since the 1930s. He asked the nation for their help in conservation, recycling, and rationing programs, and America responded generously to his pleas.

After the taxing Yalta Conference with Churchill and Stalin in February 1945, Roosevelt's physicians sent the president to his retreat in Warm Springs, Georgia, on March 30 hoping that he could relax and gain weight. Since the fall of 1944, when Roosevelt had spent nineteen days at this "little White House," the press had noted his gray pallor, weight loss, and hoarse voice. On the afternoon of Thursday, April 12, while sitting for a portrait, the president complained of a headache and became unconscious. He was moved to a nearby polio sanatorium, but never regained consciousness, and died at 3:35 P.M., in his thirteenth year in office, on the eighty-third day of his fourth term.

BEST KNOWN FOR: The New Deal and strategic leadership in World War II
FIRST JOB: Attorney
AVOCATION: Collecting stamps and coins

RITES OF PASSAGE

Although Roosevelt's fragile health was widely known, his sudden death stunned wartime America. His funeral was conducted directly with maximum veneration and minimum ostentation.

PAYING RESPECTS

Memorial services across the nation were held simultaneously with the White House services between 4:00 and 6:00 P.M. on Saturday, April 14, 1945. The only enterprises that remained operating were war plants, and even these attempted brief tributes where feasible.

Impromptu prayer and memorial services sprang up in workplaces; stores, theaters, and restaurants were closed and stock exchanges and government offices were shuttered nationwide. Radio networks abandoned their regular schedules and devoted two days to news, remembrances, memorial music, eulogies, and speeches by the deceased president. Everywhere flags flew at half-staff.

In New York City, fifty thousand people attended a tribute led by Mayor Fiorello LaGuardia in City Hall Park while another seven thousand mourners attended Episcopal services at the Cathedral of St. John the Divine, where President Roosevelt had served as a trustee for over twenty years. Francis Cardinal Spellman, archbishop of New York City, said mass at St. Patrick's to an overflowing crowd. At the nationwide memorial hour of 4:00 P.M., five hundred subway trains were halted and the city observed a minute of silence broken only by the horns of river tugboats. So strong were emotions among New Yorkers that even in the midst of a rainstorm mourners stopped, removed their hats, bowed their heads, and even knelt on the wet pavement of Times Square, paying homage to Roosevelt.

THE FUNERAL

Early on the morning of Friday, April 13, 1945, a church bell tolled in Warm Springs, Georgia, at the Polio Foundation complex that Roosevelt had helped found and where he had died the previous evening. Standing at attention, paratroopers from nearby Fort Benning had gathered alongside one thousand troops from three infantry companies and a military band to form a cortege. At the sound of the bell, the military escorted a hearse bearing the late president in his copper-lined, mahogany coffin from the polio sanitarium through the small town.

Mrs. Roosevelt, who had arrived by airplane the previous night, followed in a separate car, accompanied by the president's devoted black Scottish terrier, Fala. They slowly traveled the three miles to the train depot, where Roosevelt's coffin was placed on a train bound for Union Station in Washington, D.C. Along the way, Americans gathered on station platforms and at whistle stops in silent tribute, weeping openly or embracing in commiseration, to honor the man who had given them hope during the worst times of the Great Depression.

THE PROCESSION Shortly after ten o'clock on the morning of Saturday, April 14, 1945, the nation's new president, Harry S. Truman, arrived at Union Station to meet the inbound train carrying FDR's body. Unrecognized by the assembled crowds at the station, he boarded the last car of the funeral train to pay his respects to Mrs. Roosevelt, joined by Roosevelt's son, Brigadier General Elliott Roosevelt, and his wife; daughter Mrs. Anna Roosevelt Boettiger and her husband; three of Roosevelt's daughters-in-law; and cabinet officers and diplomats.

A Marine band then played the national anthem. The Marines presented arms and, after lifting the coffin onto a caisson, the processional moved slowly to the White House. In accordance with protocol, Roosevelt's flag-draped coffin was carried on a gun carriage drawn by seven white horses, each left horse mounted, each right one riderless. Immediately following, an outrider rode next to Mrs. Roosevelt's car, which preceded several limousines carrying President Truman and government officials. The two-mile journey took more than an hour. At least five hundred thousand people lined the parade route, many observing from rooftops and windows along the capital's stately avenues. Because Roosevelt's body was not to lie in state, the only opportunities for ordinary citizens to pay respects to their fallen president were along the processional route in the morning, or in private commemoration at the hour of his services.

Led by the District of Columbia police, the cortege, which had assembled at Union Station to greet the train, included armored troops in carriers, infantrymen in trucks, a Marine band, midshipmen from Annapolis, a Navy band, a battalion of Marines, WAVES, and SPARS. The bands played solemn tributes, including "Onward Christian Soldiers," "Adeste Fidelis," Chopin's "Funeral March," and Handel's "Dead March" from Saul. In remembrance of the commander in chief, twenty-four heavy bombers flew in formation over Roosevelt's caisson just as it reached the White House.

THE SERVICE World War II made it difficult for Roosevelt's friends, relatives, and European colleagues to attend; consequently, the White House service on Saturday, April 14, 1945, was very small. Britain's foreign secretary, Anthony Eden, was one of the few foreign dignitaries to cross the

Atlantic for the ceremonies, and only one of Roosevelt's four sons was present; the other three sons were overseas on active military duty. The family excused all thirteen grandchildren, preferring that they remember their grandfather as they had last seen him, at his fourth inauguration in January.

The flower-bedecked East Room, where the ceremony was held, accommodated two hundred mourners. Overflow guests were seated in the Blue and Green Rooms of the White House. The Episcopal bishop of Washington, the Right Reverend Angus Dun, conducted the funeral service, which began at 4:00 P.M. eastern time. One of President Roosevelt's favorite hymns, "Eternal Father Strong to Save," opened the service, followed by an invocation and biblical readings. No eulogies were given. Instead, the bishop quoted the fallen leader's famous speech from his first inauguration: "The only thing we have to fear is fear itself." Another favorite hymn, "Faith of Our Fathers," followed. The obsequies lasted twenty-five minutes, after which the mourners dispersed, and guests who were headed to Hyde Park for the burial prepared for a 10:00 P.M. departure.

FINAL RESTING PLACE The fourteen-car train from Washington to Hyde Park, New York, transported not only Roosevelt's remains but also America's most important political and military dignitaries, including President Truman and the Roosevelt family. A second train carried Supreme Court justices, and members of Congress.

Security procedures required that the exact route of the trains and their final destination—whether the station at Hyde Park or a New York Central Railway spur on the Roosevelt property—be kept secret. As a result, General George Honnen and Colonel A. J. McGehee of the U.S. Military Academy at West Point, the two officers in charge of military protocol for the funeral, did not know until the last minute at which station the funeral train would arrive.

With little more than forty-eight hours to prepare a burial service for their fallen leader, Col. McGehee coordinated a ceremony that included a battalion of randomly chosen cadets, the brigade colors, the U.S. Military Academy Band, a battery of field artillery, a black funeral caisson with seven horses, and a caparisoned black horse, the symbol of a fallen commander. The burial plot in the rose garden of Roosevelt's family home in Hyde Park, New York, had been selected by the president himself five years earlier.

The train arrived at 9:00 A.M. on Sunday, April 15, 1945. The president's nine-hundred-pound casket left the train by hearse as a twenty-one-cannon salute was initiated; the salute ended as the casket reached the open meadow below the house. Simultaneously, P-47s of the Army Air Force flew over in formation led by a B-52 Mitchell bomber.

At 10:00 A.M., in the meadow, a battalion of six hundred cadets presented honors, and as the casket was transferred to the seven-horse caisson, a bugler played "Hail to the Chief." The cadets accompanied the caisson in columns of three up the narrow path to the rose garden, while muffled drums set the pace of the march. The lane was lined by one thousand servicemen, with another three hundred servicemen standing along the interior three sides of the hemlock-walled garden. The military band played Chopin's "Funeral March" as the carriage bearing the president's remains entered the garden. Behind it were the casket bearers, representing each of the military branches, who would transfer the coffin to its burial site. Completing the cortege, a lone cadet led the riderless horse draped in black.

Following the prayer, benediction, and hymn, Franklin Delano Roosevelt's casket was lowered into its grave. An eight-gun volley rang out thrice as a final farewell and Fala, Roosevelt's Scottish terrier, barked repeatedly after each barrage. "Taps" was played, and then there was silence.

PRESIDENT ROOSEVELT IS DEAD;
TRUMAN TO CONTINUE POLICIES;

9TH CROSSES ELBE, NEARS BERLIN

U.S. AND RED ARMIES DRIVE TO MEET

WEIMAR TAKEN, RUHR POCKET SLASHED

AROUND THE WORLD

Irrespective of time zone, American military troops on both war fronts observed five minutes of silence simultaneously with the 4:00 P.M. funeral service at the White House.

In Britain, the royal court went into mourning for seven days, and France declared April 14, 1945, a national day of mourning. The British newspapers, limited by wartime rationing of paper, were permitted to print only four pages per day, three of which were devoted to memorializing Roosevelt. The Soviet Union raised its red and black mourning flag over the Kremlin, all government buildings, and many private buildings on April 14, 1945. No foreigner had ever received such an honor. In Germany, the Nazi press called Roosevelt a war criminal and referred to his death as divine justice.

BEYOND THE GRAVE

New York Telephone reported that it had its heaviest-ever volume of calls on the evening of April 12, 1945, between 5:50 and 6:45 P.M., when the news of the president's death was spreading literally by phone wire.

Upon learning of the president's death, the New York Philharmonic Symphony Society canceled its April 12, 1945, evening concert at Carnegie Hall. This was the society's second cancellation; the first was in 1865 after President Abraham Lincoln's death.

Roosevelt was not alone at the time of his death, as newspaper articles of the day had informed. Years later, it was reported that his former secretary, Lucy Mercer, who had caused a rift in his marriage to Eleanor, had been with him when he died and during his entire stay at Warm Springs. Additionally, it came to light that his daughter, Anna, had arranged for this, and numerous other, secret liaisons without her mother's knowledge.

Eleanor Roosevelt died in 1962 and is buried beside her husband. Attending her funeral were past and future U.S. presidents: Harry S. Truman, Dwight D. Eisenhower, John F. Kennedy, and Lyndon B. Johnson. Hyde Park is now maintained by the U.S. Park Service as a National Historic Site.

ODD COINCIDENCES

The day of Roosevelt's birth, January 30, is the same day of Mahatma Gandhi's death, in 1948, and Winston Churchill's funeral, in 1965.

The day of Roosevelt's death, April 12, and funeral, April 15, were shared by Josephine Baker thirty years later, in 1975.

THE HEREAFTER

In the four months after Roosevelt's death, the war in Europe and the Pacific was won and democracy triumphed. As a legacy, FDR left a blueprint for a peaceful world: a United Nations built upon four essential freedoms—Freedom from Want, Freedom from Fear, Freedom of Belief, and Freedom of Expression.

A HALF-MILLION AMERICANS LINE THE PROCESSION ROUTE ON CONSTITUTION AVENUE AS THE PRESIDENT'S COFFIN IS BROUGHT TO THE WHITE HOUSE.

BABE RUTH

"Babe"

February 6, 1895–August 16, 1948

"I honestly don't know anybody who wants to live more than I do."

➳ THE **BABE**, WITH ADMIRERS.

VITAL STATISTICS

AGE AT DEATH: 53

CAUSE OF DEATH: Thoracic cancer

SURVIVORS: His wife, Claire Hodgson; two daughters, Mrs. Richard Flanders and Mrs. Daniel Sullivan; and a sister, Mrs. Wilbur Moberly

LAST WORDS: "I'm going over the valley."

HIS LIFE

George Herman Ruth Jr., the eldest of eight children born to Maryland saloon owners, earned a reputation as a troublemaker early in life. His parents sent the seven-year-old to St. Mary's Industrial School for Boys in Baltimore, where Ruth learned not only the tailoring trade but also the game of baseball. Ruth played ball far better than he sewed, and on the recommendation of a tutor, the Baltimore Orioles signed the young left-handed pitcher in 1914.

A local sportswriter referred to the new young Orioles as "babes" and, from the tender age of nineteen, Ruth would forever be known as "Babe." The neophyte showed great promise, but financial woes forced the Orioles to trade him to the Boston Red Sox. He pitched for the Red Sox from 1914 until 1920, when they traded him to the New York Yankees for an unprecedented $125,000. Ruth demanded $20,000 a year, twice his Red Sox salary. Although the Yankees initially balked, Ruth—six feet two, barrel-chested, teetering on matchstick legs—became their best investment, packing the ballpark, winning pennants and World Series, and setting records.

The southpaw achieved renown by winning more than twenty games in both 1916 and 1917. His earned-run average was an impressive 2.28, based on eighty-nine career wins and forty-six losses. He stood as one of baseball's greatest players based on his throwing statistics alone. But after pitching only five games, the Yankees assigned the Babe to the outfield to ensure that he would bat in every game. In his first season for New York, the twenty-five-year-old slugger hit an astonishing fifty-four home runs, with a batting average of .376.

When out of Yankee pinstripes, the Babe, with his happy-go-lucky, all-consuming personality and legendary appetite for food, drink, and dames, became a media darling. Enhancing Ruth's mythical status, sportswriters competed with one another to create catchy nicknames for him, such as the "Sultan of Swat," "Rajah of Rap," "Mammoth of Maul," "Colossus of Clout," "Wali of Wallop," "Maharajah of Mash," "Mauling Mastodon," and "Blunderbuss."

The Babe continued his record-making career for the Yankees, belting sixty home runs in one season, a record that stood until 1961. He also led the league in home runs for ten years, tying it for two more. His fans attended in droves, so the Yankees eventually constructed a larger stadium in the Bronx, still used today, known affectionately as "the house that Ruth built."

Although Ruth was the highest-paid sports figure of his time, earning $80,000 in 1930, he was accessible and always considerate to his young fans. Remembering the difficulties of his own childhood, the slugger played father to thousands, regularly spending time with sick and underprivileged youngsters. The Babe married Helen Woodford in October 1914, and in 1922 the couple adopted a baby girl, Dorothy. Tragedy struck in 1929 when his wife died in a fire in their Massachusetts home.

By the mid-1920s, the Yankees had suspended Ruth more than once for drinking, being overweight, and missing practices. As his averages dipped, so did his salary. Although Ruth cleaned up his act considerably after his second marriage, to longtime mistress Claire Hodgson, he had only a few prime years left.

In 1935, the Yankees released the Babe from his contract and retired his number, "3." At age forty, he became a player-manager for the Boston Braves. But soon the Braves, too, released the unfit and wobbly Ruth. Later that year, Ruth reluctantly retired from baseball, holding fifty-four major league records and tying four more—considerably more than any other player. His lifetime home run record of 714 lasted nearly forty years.

In 1936, the Baseball Museum in Cooperstown included Ruth in the first group of players to be inducted in the Hall of Fame. Two years later, Ruth worked briefly for the Brooklyn Dodgers as a batting coach. In August 1942, forty-seven-year-old Ruth played in his pinstriped uniform one final time in a benefit game at Yankee Stadium.

Five years later, the Yankees honored the southpaw slugger by designating April 27, 1947, "Babe Ruth Day." Thousands of adoring fans hailed the Babe, who appeared before them drawn and obviously weakened by disease, leaning on a bat for support. That same year Ruth set up a charitable trust, the Babe Ruth Foundation, to continue his work on behalf of needy children. Ruth's family and friends knew that he was suffering from thoracic cancer, but they deliberately withheld information about his illness from him, hoping to encourage his recovery.

On June 13, 1948, Yankee Stadium celebrated its twenty-fifth anniversary. Ruth, the first player to have hit a home run in Yankee Stadium, attended but was too ill to play in the exhibition game. Former teammates and the public were shocked by Ruth's frail appearance. Even without knowing the exact nature of his illness, the Babe sensed that the end was near and after the game he tearfully confided to teammate Joe Duggan, "I'm gone."

Within weeks, Ruth's condition became grave, and he was admitted to New York City's Memorial Hospital on East 68th Street on June 24, 1948. Although a Catholic priest administered last rites on July 21, 1948, the Babe rallied five days later and attended the movie premiere of *The Babe Ruth Story,* starring William Bendix as the slugger; too weak to stay through the entire film, Ruth returned to the hospital. On Thursday, August 12, the *New York Times* reported in the first of a series of front page stories that the Babe's condition had become critical. Memorial Hospital issued bulletins three times a day, and President Truman and Francis Cardinal Spellman, the archbishop of New York City, checked in with the hospital staff. Fifteen thousand telegrams and letters arrived offering prayers for the Babe, and throngs of well-wishers gathered in silent vigil outside the hospital.

When the baseball legend died on August 16, his family and a priest were by his bedside. The day after Ruth's death, his family revealed that he had suffered from cancer.

BEST KNOWN FOR: His fifty-four major-league records, including 714 home runs; 2,211 runs batted in; 2,056 walks; .342 batting average; .690 slugging average; and 1,306 strikeouts

FIRST JOB: Shirt maker

AVOCATIONS: Working on behalf of disadvantaged children; writing (*How to Play Baseball,* in 1931 and *The Babe Ruth Story,* with Bob Considine, in 1948)

RITES OF PASSAGE

PAYING RESPECTS

On the evening of Monday, August 16, just as the New York Yankees were about to play the New York Giants at the Polo Grounds, the stadium announcer delivered the news of the Babe's passing to a stunned crowd. The fans rose at once, removed their hats, and observed a moment of silence before play commenced.

At the Baseball Hall of Fame, flags flew at half-staff, and black crepe was draped around Ruth's bronze induction plaque and the memorabilia case holding his glove and cap.

In praising Ruth, former president Warren G. Harding recalled that a young boy had once asked him to sign his autograph book three times, explaining to Harding, "It takes two of yours to trade for one of Babe Ruth's."

Due to the extraordinary outpouring of condolences, the Ruth family decided that the Babe should lie in state at Yankee Stadium. Arriving in a hearse a few hours after his death, Ruth's body lay in state in the rotunda under the grandstand for two days, August 17 and 18, 1948.

Mrs. Ruth and her daughter, Mrs. Richard Flanders, passed the open mahogany coffin first. Police had woefully underestimated the anticipated crowd, which swelled to seventy-seven thousand. Reporters calculated that more people walked by Babe Ruth's casket than had ever seen him play in a single game. The Babe's fans waited four, five, and six abreast for several hours as the line snaked around Yankee Stadium. At the express wish of Ruth's widow, who did not want a single admirer turned away, Yankee Stadium remained open until midnight on Tuesday, August 17, well past its scheduled closing time of 9:30. Even after locking up, guards reopened the gates so that three hundred late-arriving fans from out of state could pay their respects. The next day Yankee Stadium stayed open until 7:25 P.M.

Except for the silence, the crowds resembled those attending an ordinary baseball game. Men arrived from work in shirtsleeves, and women and children were dressed casually. Nearby a hot-dog stand served franks, and vendors sold soft drinks and souvenirs in front of the ballpark. In every way, it was very much Babe Ruth's crowd.

A twenty-six-year-old wartime amputee waiting on line recalled meeting the baseball legend when Ruth had taken him, along with 250 other children from a Poughkeepsie orphanage, to a game at Yankee Stadium: "I was only a kid, but I remember every inning as though it were yesterday; I had to see the Babe again."

THE FUNERAL

Although it rained on Friday, August 20, the day of Babe Ruth's funeral, seventy-five thousand of his admirers showed up early to stake out positions behind police barriers on Fifth Avenue. Family members and honorary pallbearers arrived well before the scheduled 11:00 A.M. services at St. Patrick's Cathedral, and 250 policemen ensured the orderly passage of their cortege. Fifty men who had been significant in the Babe's life served as honorary pallbearers, including Governor Thomas Dewey of New York; Mayor William O'Dwyer of New York City; the mayors of Baltimore and Boston; William Bendix, star of *The Babe Ruth Story;* Connie Mack, manager of the Philadelphia Athletics; Joe DiMaggio, Yankees outfielder; Joe Duggan, retired Yankees third baseman; Jack Dempsey, former heavyweight boxing champion; Brother Charles of St. Mary's Industrial School; Bill "Bojangles" Robinson, dancer; and Ed Sullivan, columnist and future television show host. Six thousand mourners filled the Fifth Avenue cathedral to capacity.

THE SERVICE In typical baseball fashion, the rain caused a delay for the services, which began with Monsignor Joseph F. Flannelly of St. Patrick's blessing the body and sprinkling holy water on the coffin. An eighteen-member male choir sang "Miserere," by Pietro Yon, while the honorary pall-bearers walked down the main aisle of the cathedral ahead of Ruth's casket. His weeping wife and two daughters followed the silver-bordered, black-pall-draped coffin and took their seats on the Gospel side of the altar.

Cardinal Spellman presided over the requiem mass, assisted by Monsignor Flannelly and forty-four priests. Eloquent moments of prayer and song punctuated the hour-long obsequies, and the cardinal delivered an inspirational prayer that began, "May the Divine Spirit that inspired Babe Ruth to overcome hardships and win the crucial game of life animate many generations of American youth."

At noon, the bereaved family exited the cathedral behind Ruth's now floral-draped coffin. The rain stopped and, in the minutes that passed while the mourners got into their cars, not a drop fell. However, as soon as the last car was readied, the heavens opened up and a deluge fell on the spectators.

THE PROCESSION The twenty-five-car cortege proceeded up Fifth Avenue, over the Walton Avenue Bridge, through the Bronx, and past Yankee Stadium en route to Westchester County's Gate of Heaven Cemetery in Hawthorne. Along the thirty-mile route another one hundred thousand of Ruth's admirers, many of them children, waited in the pouring rain to glimpse the cars as they passed. Drivers pulled their automobiles to the shoulder giving way to the cortege, and suburbanites clambered onto rooftops to see the hearse carrying baseball's most celebrated player.

FINAL RESTING PLACE Six thousand additional mourners jammed the cemetery. The cortege arrived shortly before two o'clock, and a simple ceremony marked Ruth's passage to a temporary vault. Since the family had not acquired a suitable plot, Ruth remained in the vault until the fall. On October 25, 1948, with little fanfare, Monsignor George C. Ehardt, managing director of Gate of Heaven Cemetery, officiated at the committal service for Babe Ruth. Ruth's wife and five of his friends attended the brief service.

NEWS OF THE DAY
AUGUST 17, 1948
BABE RUTH, BASEBALL IDOL, DIES AT 53 AFTER LINGERING ILLNESS

ALGER HISS TO FACE WHITIKER CHAMBERS AUGUST 25

ARREST OF 'TOKYO ROSE' ORDERED

ISRAEL ISSUES OWN CURRENCY TODAY

AUGUST 20, 1948
75,000 GO TO BABE RUTH'S FUNERAL AND STAND IN RAIN ALONG FIFTH AVE.

RUSSIAN POLICE FIRE ON GERMANS IN BERLIN STREETS

BEYOND THE GRAVE

In its front-page story on August 24, the *New York Times* reported that Babe Ruth had bequeathed part of his estate to the Babe Ruth Foundation to help the "kids of America." The Foundation in turn created the Babe Ruth Fund to raise money for children with cancer. On September 2, 1948, the Fund accepted its first two donations: $100,000 from the Revere Camera

Company of Chicago, and ten cents from thirteen-year-old Jackie Minogue of New York.

ODD COINCIDENCES

Babe Ruth shared his death date with Elvis Presley. The Home Run King and the King of Rock 'n' Roll both died on August 16, twenty-nine years apart.

The day before Ruth died, the *New York Times* ran a photograph of Joe DiMaggio safely reaching third base in a walloping 14-3 defeat of the Philadelphia Athletics. It was the second day in a row that the Yankees routed the Athletics. The next day, Ruth's family asked both Yankee Joe DiMaggio and the Athletics' octogenarian manager, Connie Mack, to serve as honorary pallbearers.

THE LINE OF MOURNERS SNAKES AROUND "THE HOUSE THAT RUTH BUILT" TO PAY THEIR RESPECTS TO THE **BABE**.

A YOUNG FAN TAKES A FINAL GLIMPSE AT THE **SULTAN OF SWAT** AS HE LIES IN STATE AT YANKEE STADIUM.

DIANA SPENCER

"Princess Di"

July 1, 1961–August 31, 1997

"Whoever is in distress can call on me. I will come running wherever they are. It is my destiny."

A SEA OF FLORAL TRIBUTES FOR
THE PRINCESS.

VITAL STATISTICS

AGE AT DEATH: 36

CAUSE OF DEATH: Heart failure from internal hemorrhaging as a result of an automobile crash

SURVIVORS: Two sons, Prince William and Prince Harry; two sisters, Lady Sarah McCorquodale and Lady Jane Fellowes; a brother, Charles, the ninth Earl Spencer; and her mother, Frances Shand Kydd

HER LIFE

The second of four children of the eighth Earl Spencer and Frances Shand Kydd, Diana Frances Spencer was born at Sandringham, Norfolk, England. When her parents divorced in 1969, Diana and her siblings remained in the custody of their father. Both parents remarried; Diana did not speak to her mother until the 1980s.

Diana's older sister, Sarah, dated the Prince of Wales, but it was Diana who won his hand. They were married with great ceremony in front of a live television audience of millions on July 29, 1981, in St. Paul's Cathedral in London. Diana was nineteen years old; her fairy-tale prince, Charles, was thirty-one.

A beautiful, blushing bride, Princess Diana appeared reticent in her first public appearances. Pregnant with Prince William after a year of marriage, she took comfort in youthful motherhood and put up with the intrusions on her privacy that come with bearing a future King of England. By the time the princess was pregnant with Prince Harry three years later, the British press reported trouble in paradise. Prince Charles had continued an earlier relationship while married. The princess suffered bouts of depression that led to bulimia and attempted suicide. Meanwhile, the marriage became fodder for the British tabloids, whose reporters stalked Princess Di relentlessly.

Kept out of the royal family's inner circle, humiliated by her husband's extramarital affair, and exposed in press photos during intimate moments, Princess Diana worked to reverse her victim role. She found the inner resources to combat her illnesses, became savvy about the press, and became a devoted and tireless champion of the poor, the sick, and those without a public voice.

After an embarrassing exchange of television interviews in which the prince and the princess each revealed unsavory private details about the marriage, Queen Elizabeth granted the royal couple a divorce, stripping Diana of the honorific "Her Royal Highness" but leaving her with the title "Princess of Wales." The House of Windsor gave Diana a $22.5 million settlement with a $600,000 yearly allowance, and she retained her apartment residence at Kensington Palace. The divorce became final on August 28, 1996.

Just one year later, tragedy struck. On a weekend sojourn in Paris, Princess Diana and her playboy companion, Dodi al Fayed, dined at the Ritz Hotel on Saturday evening, August 30, 1997. In order to avoid the paparazzi, they slipped out through a back door of the posh hotel into a waiting Mercedes S280 limousine. The photographers caught on and followed. A high-speed chase ensued, and in a tunnel underneath the Place de l'Alma on the right bank of the Seine, the Mercedes, traveling at three times the legal speed limit, careened into a concrete column dividing the roadway and ricocheted into the opposite wall at full force. Alive at the scene, the princess died a few hours later in a Paris hospital. Al Fayed and the chauffeur were killed instantly. Only al Fayed's bodyguard, Anthony Rees-Jones, survived.

French police arrested ten photographers, confiscating twenty rolls of film. Initially accused of causing the deadly accident, the photographers were vindicated by the chauffeur's toxicology report, which indicated a blood alcohol level of three times the French legal limit, and traces of prescription drugs Prozac and Tiapridal.

The crash scene was shocking. An off-duty emergency-room doctor, Frédéric Mailliez, arrived by chance only minutes after the crash and worked to save the unconscious princess, wedged between the front and back seats on the floor of the car, until the French emergency unit (SAMU) came six minutes after the accident. He did not recognize the most-photographed face in the world.

Because of the princess's delicate condition, it took nearly an hour for emergency crews to extract her from the car and stabilize her on site, and another forty minutes to take her to Pitié-Salpêtrière Hospital on the other side of town, normally a seven-minute ride. Two minutes away from the emergency room, Princess Diana suffered cardiac arrest. After two futile hours of hand-massaging her heart, doctors declared the princess dead at 4:00 A.M. Paris time on Sunday, August 31.

BEST KNOWN FOR: Her style; her compassion
FIRST JOB: Nanny
AVOCATION: Caring for those in need

RITES OF PASSAGE

Against the queen's wishes, Prince Charles, who had been awakened that morning at Balmoral Castle and told the devastating news, flew to Paris with Diana's sisters to bring her body back to England for the funeral. By the time the jet touched down shortly before seven o'clock on Sunday evening, coverage of the shocking events had preempted all other television programming.

Mohamed al Fayed flew to Paris earlier on Sunday to claim the body of his son. Muslim custom requires burial within twenty-four hours of death, and al Fayed wanted his son to be buried in England. By noon, his son's remains had been flown back to London. That same evening, August 31, Dodi al Fayed's body was wrapped in three white cloths in accordance with Muslim practice before being placed in its coffin and, after a twenty-five minute service at London's Central Mosque, was buried in the Brookwood Cemetery in Woking.

THE PREPARATION

The public outpouring of sorrow compelled Prime Minister Tony Blair to prevail upon Prince Charles and members of the House of Lords to lobby the queen for a state funeral. Her Majesty objected, as did Diana's brother, Earl Spencer. In the end, the unprecedented national grief demanded a funeral plan encompassing public tributes and private testimonials.

To the astonishment of her subjects, Queen Elizabeth did not show any outward sorrow and chose not to return to London. British newspapers admonished her with headlines such as WHERE IS OUR QUEEN? The queen was embroiled in a dilemma. If Her Majesty returned to London, the Union Jack would automatically be flown over Buckingham Palace. Not to lower the flag would have been an unthinkable affront to her grieving subjects, but the queen refused to lower the flag for her former daughter-in-law, citing lack of precedence for all except a monarch (she had not lowered it for Winston Churchill's funeral in 1965). Finally Prince Charles presented an ultimatum: either she speak to the people directly about the absence of royal response or he would do so himself. On the eve of Diana's funeral, Queen Elizabeth, in mourning dress, addressed the nation in a rare televised appearance, explaining her actions as that of a protective grandmother, saying, "We have all been trying in our different ways to cope."

That same evening, Friday, September 5, Princess Diana's oak coffin was moved from St. James's Palace to her Kensington Palace home. Enclosed with her in the casket was a photograph of her two sons that she had carried with her to France and a photograph of her father.

PAYING RESPECTS
After the autopsy in Fulham on Sunday evening, a hearse delivered Princess Diana's body to the Chapel Royal at St. James's Palace, where she would remain until the funeral six days later.

The enormity of the grief over Diana's death was astounding. In lieu of a public viewing, mourners signed books provided for them at St. James's Palace. By Wednesday, September 3, more than seven hundred and fifty thousand of Diana's admirers had waited up to twelve hours to sign condolence books, filling forty-three leather-bound tomes, seven times as many as for the hugely popular King George VI. Many left mementos—flowers, notes, stuffed animals, candies—outside the royal palaces of Buckingham, St. James, and Kensington, and at Windsor Castle and Balmoral Castle. Central London was awash in cellophane-wrapped bouquets, and the trees in Kensington Park served as shrines encircled by votive candles and flowers. During that week, florists received orders for over a million bouquets.

THE FUNERAL
More than 2.5 billion people watched the live broadcast of the events of Saturday, September 6, 1997.

THE PROCESSION Prince Charles doubled the length of the cortege route to Westminster Abbey so that it would begin at Kensington Palace and could accommodate the millions expected to pack the London streets. The crowd that had been assembling throughout the night was twenty to thirty people deep along the route. At 9:08 A.M. on Saturday, September 6, the cortege began. A horse-drawn gun carriage carried the coffin, which was draped in the red and gold Royal Standard and topped with three white floral wreaths, one of tulips from Prince William, one of lilies from the princess's brother, Earl Spencer, and one of roses from Prince Harry. On the roses was a handwritten card from the younger prince that read "Mummy."

In front of the gun carriage, Welsh Guardsmen in red uniforms rode on horseback while others walked beside the caisson on foot. A silence came over the massive crowds at Kensington Gardens and Hyde Park along the route. Bystanders tossed flowers in front of the carriage. The bells of Westminster Abbey marked the time, tolling every minute.

When the cortege arrived at St. James's Palace, Prince Charles; his sons, Prince William and Prince Harry; his father, Prince Philip; and Diana's brother, Earl Spencer, fell in behind the carriage. They were accompanied on the four-mile, two-hour procession by five hundred representatives of Princess Diana's much-loved charities.

At Buckingham Palace, Queen Elizabeth; Prince Edward; and Prince Andrew; accompanied by his ex-wife, Sarah Ferguson; and their two daughters, Princess Beatrice and Princess Eugenie, stood outside the gates. When the cortege passed, the queen bowed her head. After the queen departed the palace for the Abbey, the Union Jack was lowered to half-staff and the crowds responded with applause.

GRIEF-STRICKEN MOURNERS LOOK ON AS THE PRINCESS'S CORTEGE PASSES THROUGH LONDON.

WELSH GUARDSMEN CARRY **DIANA**'S COFFIN INTO WESTMINSTER ABBEY.

THE SERVICE At the funeral, nearly two thousand mourners inside one-thousand-year-old Westminster Abby included heads of state, royalty, family, friends, celebrities, household staff, charity workers, and volunteers with whom Diana had worked. Outside the abbey a public-address system broadcast the service to a rapt crowd. Two 355-square-foot television screens displayed the service in Hyde Park, and more than two billion people around the world watched the BBC's live telecast of the procession and service.

Celebrity attendees included opera tenor Luciano Pavarotti; Anna Wintour, editor of *Vogue;* Donatella Versace, sister of recently slain fashion designer Gianni Versace; Karl Lagerfeld, head of the House of Chanel; actors Tom Cruise and Nicole Kidman; rock star Sting; film director Steven Spielberg; pop singer Elton John; and fashion designer Ralph Lauren.

While awaiting the arrival of the cortege, the guests listened quietly to the music of Bach, Elgar, Vaughan Williams, Mendelssohn, and Dvořák. The tenor bell of Westminster was stilled at exactly 11:00 A.M., when Queen Elizabeth and the royal party entered. Minutes later twelve Welsh Guardsmen came through the Great West Door and carried Diana's casket 110 yards down the center nave and placed it on a blue catafalque. Her male family members followed and took their seats. At the express wish of the royal family, the BBC did not televise the reactions of the young princes.

The service balanced traditional and modern elements. In addition to opening with the national anthem, "God Save the Queen" (which many refrained from singing, in protest of the queen's actions), the congregation joined in singing Diana's favorite childhood hymn, "I Vow to Thee, My Country," which Prince William had requested. The Very Reverend Dr. Wesley Carr, dean of Westminster, opened the service, and Lady Sarah McCorquodale and later Lady Jane Fellowes each read poems. Soprano Lynne Dawson sang por-

tions of the Verdi *Requiem.* The congregation arose to sing the hymn, "The King of Love My Shepherd Is." Prime Minister Tony Blair read a heartfelt biblical passage on the virtues of love from a letter by St. Paul to the Corinthians, which had also been read at Charles and Diana's wedding.

Singer Elton John delivered a tender tribute when he performed a revised version of his hit song, "Candle in the Wind," which included these revised lyrics:

"Good-bye England's rose
From a country lost without your soul
Who'll miss the wings of your compassion
More than you'll ever know"

It had been Prince William's idea to ask Elton John to perform.

Earl Spencer delivered a eulogy that lashed out at the media for its relentless intrusion into his sister's private life and admonished the Windsors for their coldheartedness, to which thousands of Britons, listening to the amplified speech outside the Abbey, responded with thunderous applause clearly heard by those inside.

The congregation sang another hymn, "Make Me a Channel of Your Peace," before the archbishop of Canterbury, the Most Reverend and Right Honorable Dr. George Carey, delivered funeral prayers, followed by the congregation's recitation of the Lord's Prayer and the Blessing, and the Welsh hymn, "Guide Me, O Thou Great Redeemer." The dean of Westminster closed with the Commendation. While the congregation remained seated, the choir sang from the Orthodox Funeral Service and Shakespeare's *Hamlet* put to music by John Tavener. Pallbearers carried the casket out the central nave; at the doors they stood for a minute of silence, observed nationwide. The cortege proceeded to an awaiting hearse for the drive north to the Spencer estate for private burial services. Prince Charles and his two sons boarded a royal train for the journey.

FINAL RESTING PLACE Princess Diana's family insisted that she be buried at Althorp, the Spencers' ancestral home, away from the commotion of central London. Hundreds of thousands of spectators lined the seventy-seven mile route. The flower-strewn hearse arrived at half past three. Nearly an hour later, on a peaceful island in a small lake, Princess Diana was laid to rest at an intimate service for her sons, her brother, her two sisters, her mother, and a handful of close friends. Prince Charles represented the royal family, providing comfort for his sons.

NEWS OF THE DAY
AUGUST 31, 1997
DIANA KILLED IN A CAR IN PARIS
IN FLIGHT FROM PAPARAZZI—FRIEND DIES

U.S.–MEXICO STUDY SEES EXAGGERATION OF MIGRATION DATA

LIMERICK BURNED, ALSO FINDS A SALVE IN "ANGELA'S ASHES"

OTHER DEATHS
Mother Teresa, the Roman Catholic nun who had founded the Missionary of Charity Order and earned the 1979 Nobel Peace Prize for her work among India's impoverished classes, died of heart failure at age eighty-seven, on September 5, 1997. The same day, Princess Diana, who had visited Mother Teresa in 1984 and had been a supporter of her work, was transported in her coffin to her Kensington Palace home, dressed in a black dress she had bought but never worn, and clutching a rosary given to her by Mother Teresa. Sir George Solti, who had served for twenty-two years as the musical direc-

tor of the Chicago Symphony and won more Grammy awards than any performer in either classical or pop categories, also died on September 5, 1997, at age eighty-four in Antibes. At the time of his death, Solti was preparing to conduct a memorial concert in Diana's honor for the BBC.

AROUND THE WORLD
On Sunday, September 14, 1997, the Episcopal Diocese of New York held a memorial service for Princess Diana in Central Park in conjunction with the Cathedral of St. John the Divine. Thousands attended the afternoon service in the North Meadow, during which a lone skywriter drew a heart across the blue sky. Flowers brought to the park were donated to nursing homes throughout the city after the service.

In Washington, D.C., a memorial service was held at the National Cathedral on Saturday, September 13, 1997.

In France, visitors continued to leave flowers and notes at the Flame of Freedom sculpture above the Place de l'Alma tunnel, the site of the fatal car crash, throughout the rest of that year.

BEYOND THE GRAVE
News organizations made quick use of the Internet when news of the fatal accident emerged. Posting information as it became available, news sites fed the public's curiosity and grief, receiving millions of on-line visitors.

Many organizations canceled scheduled events during the week between Diana's death and her burial. British music industry leader EMI postponed a gala dinner celebrating its centennial. Michael Jackson canceled his sold-out concert in Belgium out of respect for the princess.

American film actor Kevin Costner had discussed with Princess Diana the possibility of her starring with him in a sequel to his film *The Bodyguard*. According to Costner, the princess had agreed to consider the part after reviewing a preliminary script; she would have been paid a fee of $10 million, which she planned to donate to charity. The revised script of *The Bodyguard II* was delivered to Costner on August 29, 1997, two days before her death.

SECRETS TO THE GRAVE

Immediately following the deaths of Princess Diana and Dodi al Fayed, rumors surfaced that al Fayed, who had bought a $200,000 ring for the princess on the day before they died, had intended to propose to her that night after dinner. Speculation continued that al Fayed and Diana had planned to make the Villa Windsor, which they had visited with an interior decorator that day, their home together. The ring was found at al Fayed's apartment.

MEMORIALS AND TRIBUTES

Cyberspace exploded with tributes to the thirty-six-year-old idol, with fans posting hundreds of Web page tributes, photographs, and virtual shrines to her memory. Years after her death, dozens of sites are still maintained as memorials.

The Diana, Princess of Wales Memorial Fund, established on September 4, 1997, collected more than $150 million in the few weeks after her death; the fund awards at least $10 million a year to applicants.

Elton John released his revised version of "Candle in the Wind," whose lyrics had been rewritten by Bernie Taupin, on September 13, 1997. More than $16 million in proceeds from the sale benefited the Diana, Princess of Wales Memorial Fund.

In the first week of September 1997, Mohamed al Fayed instructed Harrod's to turn off its signature facade lights in memory of his son and the princess. Harrod's created a memorial window featuring photographs of the couple. A year later, the famed department store repeated the memorial tribute.

A seven-mile-walk through St. James's Park, Hyde Park, Green Park, and Kensington Gardens was sanctioned and underwritten by the British government to commemorate the life of Princess Diana. Opened in July 2000, the Diana Memorial Playground and Memorial Walk Gardens cost $2.8 million. Along the pathway eighty-nine plaques mark significant events or places in Princess Diana's life. The playground, designed with a *Peter Pan* theme, contains six separate areas, a teepee camp, a musical garden, and a replica pirate ship. No member of the Windsor or Spencer families attended.

JOSEPH STALIN

"Koba"

December 21, 1879–March 5, 1953

"Sincere diplomacy is no more possible than dry water or iron wood."

STALIN, LYING IN STATE. HIS BODY WAS VIEWED BY AN ESTIMATED TWO MILLION RUSSIANS.

VITAL STATISTICS

AGE AT DEATH: 73

CAUSE OF DEATH: Respiratory and cardiac failure resulting from a cerebral hemorrhage

SURVIVORS: A son, Vassily; and a daughter, Svetlana

CLOSE CALLS: At age six, Stalin contracted a nearly fatal case of small pox, which left him with his characteristic pockmarked complexion.

HIS LIFE

Born Joseph Vissarionovich Djugashvili to a poor family in the Georgian village of Gori, Russia, the young Joseph suffered at the hand of his alcoholic father while his hardworking mother adored and pampered him. He was still a boy when his father died, and his mother toiled as a laundress to earn enough for her son to attend religious school and become a priest. Stalin enrolled in the seminary only to be expelled before his twentieth birthday for reading unauthorized books.

Prior to his expulsion, the young rebel was already participating in revolutionary activities, and after his release from the school, he devoted all of his time to organizing political rallies. He adopted his nickname "Koba," meaning "the indomitable," after a Georgian folk hero.

As a labor organizer throughout the Caucasus, Stalin became a member of the Social Democratic Party in the early twentieth century and allied himself with the radical Bolshevik wing when it split from the party in 1903, endearing himself to the Bolshevik leader, Vladimir Lenin. Stalin raised money for the party by stealing it. He was sent to and escaped from jail on several occasions, each time returning to Lenin to work for the party.

In 1912, Lenin appointed the twenty-three-year-old Stalin to the Bolshevik Central Committee, assuring him a central power base. He became the first editor of *Pravda,* the official party newspaper, and he began using his adopted surname, Stalin, meaning "man of steel." After being exiled to Siberia for four years by the last czarist regime, Stalin reemerged after the 1917 revolution as a key player for the Bolsheviks. In 1922, he became general secretary of the Communist Party's Central Committee, reassigning party officials at will, while controlling appointments and agendas of the committee.

Stalin's lust for power and disdain for intellectuals became increasingly apparent. When Lenin died in 1924, Stalin used the power of the party's apparatus to crush his left-wing and right-wing opponents and emerge as the singular choice for Soviet leader. Leon Trotsky and his leftist followers, as well as the right-wing acolytes of Nicolay Bukharin, lost their party posts.

Upon seizing control of Russia, Premier Stalin concentrated on collective agriculture and industrialization. Known as "five-year plans," his efforts to modernize the nineteenth-century agrarian economy caused the death of millions of peasants through murder, starvation, and torture. From 1928 to 1941, he systematically annihilated middle-class farmers and peasants who did not want to serve on collectives or give up their farming traditions. In 1936, he began to purge the party of members whom he deemed disloyal, accusing them of doubtful crimes and subjecting them to false trials and executions. His long arm of retribution reached deep into the heart of the general populace. Millions died at the hands of Stalin's notorious secret police or perished in his Siberian concentration camps, punished for sometimes dubious crimes that were either ideological in nature or suspected as such.

By the time World War II erupted on the Soviet Union's western front, Stalin's reputation as a brutal tyrant was well established. Yet, his authoritative command of the Soviet army impressed the Allies, as did his conversion of Soviet industrial plants to the manufacture of armaments at a time when Britain and the United States were lagging in military production. Ironically, this helped to redeem Stalin's image in Russia and abroad. His troops kept Germany occupied, but millions of Russian soldiers perished in the war. Stalin's oldest son, Jacob, died in a German prisoner-of-war camp.

But Winston Churchill and Franklin Roosevelt remained wary, and when Stalin expanded his reach into Eastern Europe after the war, fears of Communism and atomic warfare developed. While a beleaguered free Europe watched helplessly, Stalin ushered in the Cold War by creating an Eastern Bloc of Soviet-dependent countries, including Romania, Poland, Yugoslavia, East Germany, Czechoslovakia, and Bulgaria, lurking behind what Churchill dubbed "the Iron Curtain."

The Soviet Union suffered further under Stalin's post-war regime. The paranoid dictator continued to purge the Communist Party and the government of suspected traitors near the end of his life, distrusting even his closest advisors.

On Monday, March 2, 1953, Stalin suffered a cerebral hemorrhage that left him unconscious and paralyzed on the right side. In the days that followed, he suffered repeated respiratory and cardiac failures, and he died at the Kremlin on March 5, 1953, at 9:50 P.M., in the presence of his family and several close Central Committee and Presidium members.

BEST KNOWN FOR: His reign of terror
FIRST JOB: Revolutionary agitator
AVOCATION: Singing

RITES OF PASSAGE

Communist Party officials kept news of Stalin's death secret for nearly six hours in order to close ranks and prepare an official statement. The radio news made an officially sanctioned pronouncement to the Russian people as they headed for work. The black-bordered front page of *Pravda,* the government-run newspaper, featured a full-page photograph of the premier who had ruled the Soviet Union with ultimate power.

THE PREPARATION

On Friday, March 6, grieving Muscovites began to gather in Red Square in silent tribute. The Communist Party designated the Hall of Columns in the House of Trade Unions the site where Stalin's body would lie in state, in the same room where Lenin had lain in 1924. By early morning, workers had draped the exterior of the House with black-bordered red Soviet flags, the official symbol of mourning, on either side of a gilt-framed, forty-foot-high portrait of Stalin.

Less than twelve hours after the official death announcement, family and friends followed Stalin's coffin from the Kremlin to its place of honor in the Hall of Columns. Soviet leaders Georgi Malenkov, Vyacheslav Molotov, Nikolay Bulganin, Lavrenti Beria, and Kliment Voroshilov watched over the bier in the first hours before the public was admitted while an orchestra in the room played Chopin's "Funeral March."

PAYING RESPECTS

At four o'clock, the public entered through the massive wooden doors to see the great Soviet dictator. Illuminated by floodlights, Stalin was dressed in his gray military uniform adorned with medals; additional ribbons rested on a silk cushion by his feet. Silence gripped the room during the entire sixty hours of viewing. An estimated 2 million Russians filed past their ruthless leader, often eight abreast, before the Monday funeral.

On the second day of viewing, Saturday, March 7, the diplomatic corps in Moscow, led by the Chinese delegation, paid tribute to Stalin, arriving en masse and presenting a wreath on behalf of all foreign missions. Floral tributes from all over the world and from many Soviet collectives, factories, workers' unions, and military units blanketed an entire wall in the great hall.

The Soviet government ordered that artillery barrages be fired on Monday, March 8, at noon, the hour of Premier Stalin's burial, in Moscow, Leningrad, Sevastopol, Odessa, Kalingrad, Lvov, Khabarovsk, and Vladivostok as well as in the capitals of all Soviet republics. Additionally, the government specified that "at 12:00 noon precisely, work in all enterprises and traffic of railways, sea, and motor transport throughout the territory of the Soviet Union . . . is to be suspended five minutes."

The government also announced its intention to build a memorial shrine for Joseph Stalin and his predecessor, Vladimir Lenin, and other Soviet heroes buried beneath the Kremlin wall. This pantheon was to have replaced Lenin's red-and-black marble tomb that has sat in Red Square since 1924, but it was never constructed.

THE FUNERAL

THE PROCESSION On the morning of Monday, March 9, after two and a half days of lying in state, Stalin received an official state funeral. By eight o'clock, more than fifty thousand civilians had filled Red Square. At ten o'clock, two blocks away, new Soviet premier Georgi Malenkov helped carry Stalin's coffin out of the Hall of Columns and onto a waiting gun caisson. The Chinese premier and foreign minister, Zhou Enlai, joined him and other honorary pallbearers.

The procession contained the solemn elements that had become expected of grand Soviet ceremonies in Red Square: military displays, punctuality, rhetoric, and party solidarity. Accompanied by Chopin's "Funeral March," the cortege, followed by flower bearers with colorful wreaths, took twenty minutes to reach Red Square. The fourteen marshals of the Soviet Union, each carrying one of Stalin's medals on a crimson cushion, preceded a riderless horse, which in turn was followed by the six-horse team pulling Stalin's coffin on a military-green gun caisson. The Soviet leadership and Stalin's family followed the coffin and were accompanied by diplomatic representatives.

THE SERVICE During his twenty-nine years in power, Stalin, with his fellow leaders, had frequently stood atop Lenin's tomb reviewing troops, receiving tributes, and delivering speeches. The procession stopped in front of the mausoleum and the Soviet leaders mounted Lenin's tomb as they had done many times before, this time in preparation for delivering their funeral orations. Stalin's casket was moved from the caisson to a central bier in front of the tomb.

In a telling eulogy, the fifty-one-year-old Malenkov promised the Soviet people peace and a better standard of living. Lavrenti Beria, the new interior minister, and Vyacheslav Molotov, the new foreign minister, delivered speeches supporting Malenkov and leaving the impression that Soviet national unity was assured.

FINAL RESTING PLACE Descending from the podium, the three leaders joined Nikita Khrushchev, Nikolay Bulganin, and Lazar Kaganovich at the base of the tomb to hoist Stalin's black-and-red draped coffin onto their shoulders for the final ceremony. The six men carried their fallen dictator into the crypt, placing him on Lenin's left.

Soldiers in a brief parade showcasing Soviet military strength marched in front of the tomb. Overhead a single Soviet bomber, followed by a squadron of jets, flew in tribute. As the noon hour approached, cannons unleashed a deafening roar of thirty salvos, ten per minute. Factory whistles all over Moscow wailed in the quiet left by the cannons' echo. Malenkov ventured into the tomb one last time to say farewell as the Soviet band in the Red Square played Ginka's "Hail to the Russian People."

Stalin shared Lenin's mausoleum until 1961, when he was removed and buried near the Kremlin Wall. A plaque now marks the spot where Stalin was originally interred. What will be done with Lenin's remains is unclear; his body has deteriorated over time, requiring repeated restorations, the last in April 1999. Sporting a new suit and tie, Lenin was returned to his glass-enclosed tomb and remains on public view in the Red Square.

NEWS OF THE DAY

MARCH 6, 1953
STALIN DIES AFTER 29-YEAR RULE;
HIS SUCCESSOR NOT ANNOUNCED;
U.S. WATCHFUL, EISENHOWER SAYS

POLE FLIES TO DENMARK IN FIRST INTACT
RUSSIAN MIG-15 TO REACH WEST

OTHER DEATHS

Sergei Prokofiev, the celebrated Russian composer of modern symphonic music, died on March 8, 1953—the day of Stalin's entombment—in Moscow of a cerebral hemorrhage at age sixty-one. He was one of three Russian composers who had been denounced by Stalin's regime in February 1948.

AROUND THE WORLD

Official condolences from U.S. officials were respectful, due to the premier's role during World War II. However, the Cold War had left the United States with an uncomfortable relationship with the Communist ruler, and outward signs of mourning were visible only at the United Nations, where its flag flew at half-staff.

In Britain, former prime minister Winston Churchill was diplomatic but impersonal in his message of condolence to the Soviet Union. In France, however, the French premier delivered a eulogy to the Parliament and ordered that the tricolor flag be lowered in respect for the Soviet premier.

The East German government wrapped many of its buildings in black crepe and lowered the East German and Soviet flags. The statue of the dictator in Stalin Allee received multitudes of floral memorials and became the focus of affection for the fallen premier.

Mao Zedong declared three days of official mourning for Premier Stalin, ordering the Chinese flag to be flown at half-staff. Prime Minister Jawaharlal Nehru of India declared two minutes of silence at the opening of Parliament and had the flags lowered on official buildings for the day.

BEYOND THE GRAVE
ODD COINCIDENCES

On March 6, the day that Stalin's death was announced, pilots from McCord Air Force Base carried out a mock air attack over Shelton, Washington, using two F-80 jet fighters. The fighter planes screaming over the town caused residents to run in panic, thinking the Soviets were now at war with the United States.

MYSTERIOUS CIRCUMSTANCES

Stalin's daughter claimed to have witnessed her father's agonizing death not in Moscow, but in a small hamlet six miles from the city. She reported that Stalin, struggling for breath in his painful last moments, realized that the very men responsible for caring for his health might have poisoned him. In a final gesture, he pointed to the ceiling as if to invoke the wrath of God. "The Doctor's Plot," as it was subsequently known, was exposed as a fabrication during Khrushchev's de-Stalinization period.

THE HEREAFTER

Georgi Malenkov succeeded Joseph Stalin as the Soviet premier and was followed briefly by Bulganin and later by Nikita Khrushchev, who distanced himself from Stalin's reign of terror. In the 1980s, under the open policy of glasnost, then-Soviet leader Mikhail Gorbachev admitted that Stalin's rule had been replete with reprehensible crimes. New evidence indicates that Stalin slaughtered as many as 25 to 30 million Russian people during his twenty-nine-year regime.

↝ SOVIET LEADERS CARRY **STALIN**'S COFFIN INTO RED
SQUARE. FROM LEFT: NIKOLAY BULGANIN, VYACHESLAV MOLOTOV,
VASSILY STALIN, GEORGI MALENKOV, AND LAVRENTI BERIA.

IGOR STRAVINSKY

"Bubushkin"

June 17, 1882–April 6, 1971

"I have been offered as much to appear on a TV talk show—or was it "What's My Line?"— as I have earned from my entire life work as a composer."

∿ **IGOR STRAVINSKY** COMPOSING THE *REQUIEM CANTICLES,* WHICH WOULD LATER SERVE AS THE MUSIC FOR HIS OWN FUNERAL.

VITAL STATISTICS

AGE AT DEATH: 88

CAUSE OF DEATH: Heart failure

SURVIVORS: His widow, Vera de Bosset; a daughter, Mrs. Milene Marion; two sons, Theodore and Soulima; and a granddaughter, Kitty

HIS LIFE

Born on St. Igor's Day in June 1882 outside of St. Petersburg, Igor Fyodorovich Stravinsky was the third son of a Russian bass singer with the Imperial Opera. Showing an early musical ability, a talent that his parents did not appreciate, the young man studied law in exchange for permission to also pursue music composition while at the University of St. Petersburg.

There he studied with Russian composer Nikolay Rimsky-Korsakov, under whom he composed and performed his first orchestral work, the *Scherzo Fantastique*. Later that year, Stravinsky met the Russian ballet impresario Sergey Diaghilev, who commissioned him to write a ballet, *Les Sylphides*, based on two of Chopin's piano works.

Diaghilev and Stravinsky collaborated on many ballets for the Ballets Russes, the most celebrated of which, *L'Oiseau de Feu* (The Firebird), launched the composer into musical notoriety. Composed in 1909, the orchestral suite became his most recognized work. The next ballet Stravinsky wrote for Diaghilev's troupe was a breakthrough in modern sound. *Petrushka* used bitonality for the first time, and the simultaneous use of two musical keys became known as the "*Petrushka* chord." With ballet star and choreographer Vaslav Nijinsky dancing the title role, the Ballet Russes's summer season at the Paris Opera House in 1911 shook the creative world.

That world became nearly hysterical when, in May 1913, the company premiered *Le Sacre du Printemps* (The Rite of Spring) with Nijinsky as choreographer—the audience rioted in response to Stravinsky's avant-garde music and the ballet's modern dance style. Henceforth Stravinsky's music became widely known as the harbinger of great artistic trends in the twentieth century.

With his first wife, Catherine Nossenko, a distant cousin whom he married in 1906, and two children, Stravinsky moved to Europe before the start of World War I and became estranged from his homeland after the Russian Revolution of 1917. He settled in Paris and produced several additional significant compositions during a creative phase referred to as his "Dionysian" period. Diaghilev remained his primary patron for nearly twenty years.

During the war, Stravinsky streamlined his writing style, composing *L'Histoire du Soldat* (The Soldier's Tale) in 1918 for just seven instruments so that musicians performing it could tour easily and economically. The work reflected the influence of jazz, the popular musical style of the time, as did his next piece, *Ragtime*. Having written these two pieces in a pared-down style, Stravinsky appropriated the style for his next creative period between the two world wars, which came to be called his "neoclassical" phase.

Stravinsky was a strong creative force in Paris, cultivating relationships with poet Jean Cocteau, painter Pablo Picasso, writer André Gide, and choreographer George Balanchine. He wrote *Pulcinella* in 1920 for Diaghilev, and in 1927 he created another sensation with *Oedipus Rex,* an oratorio composed for an American tour, whose libretto was written by Cocteau. A ballet composed only for strings commissioned by Elizabeth Sprague Coolidge, *Apollon Musagété* (Apollo), again broke new ground.

In 1938, his eldest daughter, Ludmilla, died of tuberculosis, and a year later his wife died of the same disease. At age fifty-seven Stravinsky moved to the United States, where he felt his music was better understood. The painter Vera de Bossett, his mistress, accompanied him. In Boston, Stravinsky taught at Harvard University as the Charles Eliot Norton Professor of Poetry, delivering a series of lectures in French on the art of composition, which he later expanded upon in his 1948 book, *Poetics of Music.*

He moved to Los Angeles in 1942 and composed a chamber piece, *Danses Concertantes,* for the Werner Janssen Symphony Orchestra, and *Orpheus,* a ballet commissioned by George Balanchine. It was well known that Stravinsky would only compose when well paid for his work. Regardless of his cerebral style of music, he accepted a commission from Ringling Brothers and Barnum and Bailey Circus in 1942 to write the "Circus Polka," to which an elephant performed under the big top. In the 1950s he worked on his third opera, *The Rake's Progress,* with a libretto by Chester Kallman and the poet W. H. Auden.

During his later years in the United States, Stravinsky began to move away from neoclassicism and toward serial music, a style that had been popularized by his contemporary, Arnold Schoenberg.

Born into the Russian Orthodox religion, Stravinsky left the church as a young man but returned to it in Europe where he attended regular services, and throughout his career wrote a number of inspired pieces of religious music including *Symphony of Psalms* (1930), *Canticum Sacrum* (1956), and *Threni* (1958). *Requiem Canticles* (1966) later served as his own funeral music.

Stravinsky had written an autobiography in 1938 and, in addition to *Poetics of Music,* wrote six more books between 1958 and 1969, exposing his innermost thoughts on composition and music criticism while giving light to anecdotes, humor, and trivialities from his life. He returned to Russia in 1962, at the age of eighty, not having seen his homeland since before World War I. In 1969 he moved to New York City with Vera, now his wife.

Frail since suffering several arterial strokes beginning in 1967, Stravinsky was admitted to Lenox Hill Hospital in New York City in March 1971 for pulmonary edema and was released just a week before his death. His wife reported that he was mentally active, listening to the recorded music she played for him on the stereo. He died at his apartment at 920 Fifth Avenue at 5:20 A.M. on Tuesday, April 6, 1971. At his side were his wife; his faithful musical assistant, Robert Craft; and his personal manager, Lillian Libman.

BEST KNOWN FOR: *The Firebird*
FIRST JOB: Law student
AVOCATION: Collecting books and record albums

RITES OF PASSAGE

Upon Stravinsky's passing, critic Herbert Read offered perhaps the ultimate praise: "It is given to some, whatever their craft, to be in virtue of their universality the representative artist of their age—a Dante, a Shakespeare, a Michelangelo, a Goethe. The most representative artist of our own Twentieth Century has been, not a poet or a painter, but a musician—Igor Stravinsky."

THE PREPARATION

Six months prior to his death, Stravinsky decided that he wanted to be buried in the Russian section of the cemetery on the island of San Michele in Venice, a decision he attributed to listening to his own *Requiem Canticles.*

PAYING RESPECTS

Family members and close friends attended private services on Tuesday and Wednesday, April 6 and 7, 1971, at the Frank E. Campbell Funeral Chapel in New York City.

On learning the news of Stravinsky's death, the New York Philharmonic Orchestra dedicated its weekly musical program to the master, unable to change its scheduled performances. The New York City Opera dedicated its April 6 performance of *Don Rodrigo* to Stravinsky.

THE FUNERAL

On Friday, April 9, 1971, hundreds of Stravinsky's fans waited for hours on line outside the funeral home, hoping to get a seat in the chapel where services would be held. Those unable to get inside stood in the lobby, straining to hear the service.

THE SERVICE In the front pews, stars of the international musical world stood throughout most of the Russian Orthodox service, including violinist Isaac Stern, conductor Leopold Stokowski, opera singer Marilyn Horne, and pianist Arthur Rubinstein. Both President Richard Nixon and the Russian ambassador sent representatives to the funeral. Stravinsky's family members, seated in the front row, held white candles.

The forty-minute service featured traditional hymns from the Russian Orthodox liturgy as well as chorale music written by Stravinsky, including his songs "Paternoster" and "Ave Maria." The Reverend Alexander Schmemann, dean of St. Vladimir's Theological Seminary in Crestwood, New York, conducted the service in both English and Russian. The choir from the seminary intoned Russian chants, singing "Gospodi pomilyi" ("Lord have mercy") and closing with "viechnaya parmiat" ("eternal memory"). At the request of the family, no eulogies were delivered.

On Monday, April 12, Vera Stravinsky, Robert Craft, and two friends accompanied the composer's body on a flight to Rome, Italy. The following day, a hearse sent by the city council of Venice transported Stravinsky's remains to the city. Traveling under a blanket of red and white roses bearing the words "Riposa in Pace" ("Rest in Peace"), Stravinsky's closed mahogany coffin was ferried through the canals of Venice to the Church of San Giovani e Paolo. There the composer lay in state on Wednesday, April 14, so that Venetians could pay respects.

On Thursday, April 15, Stravinsky enjoyed a musical send-off in the historic church where Venetian magistrates have received their final obsequies for centuries. The mayor of Venice lauded the composer, quoting from his work and that of the poet Ezra Pound, who was present in the church. Robert Craft, Stravinsky's close friend and musical associate, conducted the Venice Theater's orchestra in playing Stravinsky's 1966 composition, *Requiem Canticles.* Members of the Italian Radio Choir accompanied the orchestra. Archimandrite Cheruin Malissianos of the Greek Orthodox Church conducted the religious services, which included the lighting of incense and intoning of chants. At the end of the service the coffin and floral tributes were carried across an open square to the canal where a gondola hearse received them.

THE PROCESSION Four gondoliers, dressed in traditional black pants and white shirts, silently pulled the boat carrying Stravinsky's coffin across the Grand Canal to the cemetery island of San Michele. Family members followed in gondolas. There the archimandrite sang a burial service in a tiny chapel, and Igor Stravinsky's casket was carried a few yards and lowered into the grave.

FINAL RESTING PLACE Stravinsky is buried in the Greek Orthodox section of San Michele Cemetery near the grave of his friend Sergey Diaghilev, the founder of the Ballets Russes.

NEWS OF THE DAY
APRIL 7, 1971
IGOR STRAVINSKY, THE COMPOSER, DEAD AT 88

PACIFICATION PUSH BEGUN IN VIETNAM

DALEY WINS FIFTH TERM IN CHICAGO BY A BIG MAJORITY

3 RADICALS APPEAR VICTORS IN BERKELEY CITY ELECTION

AROUND THE WORLD
In London, concerts of Stravinsky's ballet music were performed for seven days beginning at noon on Sunday, April 11, 1971, at St. Paul's Church, Covent Gardens. A memorial to Stravinsky painted by British artist David Hockney sat on the altar. Attendees brought flowers and other tributes to the service.

 In the May 15, 1971, issue of the *New York Times,* an article by Harold Schonberg reporting on the New York Philharmonic's memorial program to Stravinsky ran next to an ad for the Ringling Brothers and Barnum and Bailey Circus, a cheeky reminder that, in addition to his lofty compositions, the revered composer had once composed for that very circus.

BEYOND THE GRAVE
Stravinsky was a renowned hypochondriac who practiced calisthenics, which included walking on his hands, every morning until age sixty-seven.

The film actor Edward G. Robinson sponsored Igor Stravinsky for naturalization, assisting him in becoming an American citizen in December 1945.

The composer with the oversize talent was five feet three inches tall and weighed 120 pounds.

ODD COINCIDENCES
At the June 17, 1979, premiere of Covent Gardens's production of *The Rake's Progress,* the gold wedding band thrown into the audience by the main character, Baba the Turk, landed in the lap of Stravinsky's widow, as though the composer himself had willed it there, on what would have been his ninety-seventh birthday.

IGOR STRAVINSKY'S GONDOLA HEARSE,
FOLLOWED BY A GONDOLA CARRYING HIS WIDOW AND SON
MAKES ITS WAY DOWN THE VENICE CANAL, APRIL 15TH, 197

RUDOLPH VALENTINO

"The Sheik"

May 6, 1895–August 23, 1926

"I am merely the canvas on which women paint their dreams."

RIOTS OUTSIDE THE FUNERAL CHAPEL, WHERE **RUDOLPH VALENTINO** LAY IN STATE CONTINUED INTO THE PARLOR, WHICH WAS LOOTED BY BEREAVED FANS DESPERATE FOR SOUVENIRS.

VITAL STATISTICS

AGE AT DEATH: 31

CAUSE OF DEATH: Ruptured abdomen and infection of the heart tissues after surgery for appendicitis and gastric ulcers

SURVIVORS: His estranged second wife, film star Natacha Rambova; a brother, Alberto Guglielmi; and a sister, Maria Guglielmi

LAST WORDS: "Don't worry, Chief, I'll be all right" (spoken to Joseph Schenck, Chairman of the Board of United Artists Corporation, two hours before slipping into a coma from which he never emerged).

HIS LIFE

Rudolph Valentino, the quintessential screen idol, won celebrity status by playing flamboyant, sexual roles in a new medium that exploited sensuality, projecting an exotic sex appeal that by today's standards seems effeminate, yet caused girls to faint and women to fantasize. Journalist H. L. Mencken observed that Valentino was like "catnip to women."

The handsome actor was born Rodolfo Alfonzo Raffaelo Pierre Filibert Guglielmi di Valentina, in Castellaneta, Italy. In 1913, he immigrated to the United States, landing in New York state, where he worked in a variety of menial jobs, including gardener, handyman, and waiter, before finding work as a dancer. He graduated to teaching dance, specializing in the tango, between 1914 and 1916.

Valentino then headed to California, taking bit parts in Hollywood films under the name "Rudolpho Valentina." His first success, the 1921 silent movie, *The Four Horsemen of the Apocalypse*—featuring a tango scene—launched his career and led to *The Sheik* (also in 1921), which secured his arrival as a smoldering screen idol and "Latin Lover." His role opposite Gloria Swanson in 1922's *Beyond the Rocks* assured his position as a full-fledged Hollywood star; he appeared in thirty-three movies during his five-year film career.

In 1919, Valentino married Jean Acker, an actress of ambiguous sexual persuasion who deserted him on their wedding night. After the couple divorced, he married Natacha Rambova (formerly Winifred Hudnut), a menacing woman whose bullying of "the Sheik"—as Valentino was sometimes called—was salaciously recounted in the tabloid press. Valentino's manliness was increasingly open to question, as the star played increasingly effete roles at Rambova's insistence. In 1924's *Monsieur Beaucaire,* although he played the lead, his role, in one critic's stinging description, was that of a "painted pansy." Rambova and Valentino separated in 1925.

Valentino went on to make four more films, and in 1925 he was voted by movie exhibitors as the number one box-office draw, beating out Mary Pickford and Douglas Fairbanks, his sensual style derided by the critics but embraced by female fans. His last film, *The Son of the Sheik,* which critics considered his best work, was released just one month before his death.

What should have been a routine operation for gastric ulcers and appendicitis on August 15, 1926, resulted in his tragic death a week later. In all probability, Valentino waited too long for surgery, and the infection, unstoppable by the medicine of the time, had progressed too far. Rambova was in Europe on a shoot, but Valentino's first wife, Jean Acker, kept in touch with the

Polyclinic Hospital in Manhattan via phone from Los Angeles, as did Pola Negri, a Polish actress who claimed to be engaged to the silent star. In addition to United Artists chairman Joseph Schenck, who visited Valentino on the day of his death, Valentino's manager, S. George Ullman, remained near the star during his hospital stay.

On the morning of Sunday, August 22, 1926, Valentino's strength began to give out. Father Joseph M. Cangedo, who had grown up with Valentino in Italy, administered the Catholic last rites. The actor recovered temporarily, but the hospital summoned Father Leonard of nearby St. Malachy's church the next morning, Monday, August 23, when the actor's condition worsened. Early that morning Valentino said to his physician, Dr. Meeker, "I'm afraid we won't go fishing together. Perhaps we will meet again. Who knows?" He then talked with Schenck. After early that morning, the actor began to speak only in blurted Italian, unintelligible to the hospital staff. He slipped into a coma at eight o'clock and died at 12:10 P.M.

BEST KNOWN FOR: His smoldering on-screen persona
FIRST JOB: Gardener
AVOCATION: Farming

RITES OF PASSAGE

Fans gathered outside the hospital as soon as Valentino took ill, waiting for bulletins on the star's well-being. The crowd became unruly upon hearing the news of his death, and the hospital staff were forced to call the police to restore order.

After the actor died, medical personnel placed his body in a plain wicker casket, covered by a gold cloth, which they carried unobserved out the hospital's side door on Fifty-first Street. A van transported it to the Campbell Funeral Parlor on Sixty-sixth Street and Broadway. After a time, the crowd of mourners realized they had been duped and, discovering the star's whereabouts, charged up Broadway to the funeral parlor.

THE PREPARATION

Joseph Schenck wired Alberto Guglielmi, Rudolph Valentino's brother and next of kin. Guglielmi, who was in Paris at the time, boarded the first ship headed for the United States, hoping to arrive in time for the funeral.

According to New York Health Department code, burials at that time were required to occur within seven days of death, which in Valentino's case meant burial would have to take place by Monday, August 30. His brother, aboard the ocean liner *Homeric,* would not arrive until August 31. The health department granted Valentino's manager a forty-eight-hour extension for burial, but the funeral was not postponed.

Valentino's purported fiancée, actress Pola Negri, took to her bed in illness upon hearing the news of her lover's death, with every detail of her health and travel arrangements to the funeral being recounted in the daily newspaper. She wanted him buried in Hollywood, she said, because "he spent so many happy hours—his happiest hours—here and because I am here."

PAYING RESPECTS

According to the New York City police commissioner, he had never seen, in his twenty years of service on the force, a crowd as unruly as the one that gathered to mourn Rudolph Valentino that Tuesday, August 24, outside the funeral home. On confirmation that a viewing would begin that afternoon, the crowd—mostly women and girls—grew to ten thousand, bringing traffic on Broadway and neighboring streets to a standstill.

At two o'clock, two hours ahead of schedule and before the arrival of additional police reinforcements, the funeral home opened its doors and the crowd surged forward, shoving police officers through Campbell's plate-glass window. The crowd also shattered a store window at an auto rental agency one block away. The police, soon reinforced with mounted units, drove their horses into the crowd but failed to disperse it. In the ensuing chaos, the mob overturned an automobile, and more than one hundred people were wounded, either in the general stampede or by broken glass. Medical personnel set up a temporary hospital on the ground floor of the funeral home.

Inside the Campbell Funeral Parlor, the scene was equally unruly. Mourners snatched souvenirs—anything and everything—from the funeral home's special "Gold" room where Valentino lay in state, and employees moved the star's body to a smaller and more governable upstairs parlor. Here, Valentino's bier was marked with candles at the head and foot of his coffin, with two large rose bouquets as a backdrop. Even in this more tranquil environment, mourners fainted upon seeing the pale silent film actor laying in his bronze and silver casket. By the time the funeral parlor closed its doors at midnight more than thirty thousand people had come to pay tribute to Hollywood's premier matinee idol.

After midnight, ten black-shirted members of future Italian despot Benito Mussolini's Fascist Party arrived at the funeral home to demand that they be allowed to "stand guard" over the body, which they did, two at a time and in two-hour shifts, throughout his lying in state, leaving only at closing time.

The unruly crowd still outside the funeral home at midnight resisted police efforts to disperse them, and the next morning thousands of fans returned to stand vigil the next morning, Wednesday, August 25. Valentino's manager,

who'd had enough, canceled further public viewing of the body. "They showed gross irreverence," he said. "I am sorry they were allowed to see him at all." Thereafter, only friends and family of the screen star were admitted. By the time Valentino's body was removed, more than one hundred thousand people had waited, some in the rain, to pay their respects.

On Thursday, August 26, the curious and the loyal came out for a third day of vigil. By now, two hundred New York City policemen were on patrol in the vicinity of the funeral parlor. However, at midnight, Rudolph Valentino's coffin was closed for the final time until his brother's arrival from Italy.

Floral tributes poured in from Hollywood celebrities. Charlie Chaplin sent a wreath of orchids; Gloria Swanson, a bouquet of 150 American Beauty roses; Irving Berlin and his bride, red and white roses; Joseph Schenck and his wife, yellow roses; and Samuel Goldwyn, dahlias and still more roses.

In California, on Friday, August 27, members of "the Breakfast Club," a group of horseback riders who rode the trails of the Hollywood Hills, honored their friend and co-member in a morning ride led by Valentino's horse, which bore the star's empty boots reversed in its stirrups.

THE FUNERAL
THE PROCESSION The cortege left the funeral parlor at 10:48 A.M. on Monday, August 30, and drove down Broadway to Forty-ninth Street before a crowd of six thousand onlookers. More than 250 policemen were assigned to cortege duty and 12 motorcycle officers preceded the funeral procession to its destination. As a precaution, two medical clinics were set up on the route.

Valentino's manager appointed fourteen honorary pallbearers, including Joseph Schenck and actor Douglas Fairbanks. The Italian ambassador to the

United States was invited, but he declined. Five hundred invitation-only guests comprised an illustrious audience of stars of the day, including Pola Negri, Mary Pickford, Norma and Constance Talmadge, Gloria Swanson, George Jessel, and Clifton Webb, as well as magician Harry Houdini.

The Roman Catholic requiem mass featured soloists from the Chicago Civic Opera Company and the San Carlo Opera Company, and a choir accompanied by a sextet. Chopin's "Funeral March" marked the solemn transport of Valentino's coffin from the church to the hearse.

FINAL RESTING PLACE When Valentino's brother finally arrived in Manhattan on the afternoon of Tuesday, August 31, he resolved that his brother should be buried in Hollywood rather than in his Italian hometown. On Thursday, September 2, Valentino's body departed Grand Central Terminal encased in two caskets: a bronze and silver one inside another of bronze and gold. Blanketed in a gold cloth embellished with gladioli, larkspurs, and snapdragons, the deceased silent-screen star was secured in a special railway car.

In order to avoid mob scenes like the ones surrounding the funeral on the East Coast, the actor's manager arranged for the coffin to be unloaded at Richfield Station, outside of Los Angeles. On Monday, September 6, a police escort and a hearse met the train and carried Guglielmi and Ullman to the funeral parlor, while another car drove Negri to the Ambassador Hotel.

At ten o'clock the next morning, at the Church of the Good Shepherd in Beverly Hills, movie-industry titans attended a second invitation-only funeral tribute. Out of respect for the fallen actor, all of Hollywood's studios shut down during the hour of Valentino's funeral. No incidents disrupted the service, and that afternoon Rudolph Valentino came to his final rest in a vault at the Hollywood Forever Cemetery.

NEWS OF THE DAY

AUGUST 24, 1926
CALLIZO, FRENCH FLIER, RISES 41,811 FEET, WORLD'S RECORD

VALENTINO PASSES WITH NO KIN AT SIDE; THRONGS IN STREET

AUGUST 25, 1926
THOUSANDS IN RIOT AT VALENTINO BIER; MORE THAN 100 HURT

MANIAC BLOWS UP PITTSBURGH BANK; DIES WITH OFFICER

AUGUST 31, 1926
SILENT CROWDS SEE VALENTINO CORTEGE; SCREEN STARS WEEP

ALL CITY OFFICIALS IN ITALY LOSE JOBS

OTHER DEATHS

Peggy Scott, a twenty-seven-year-old British actress, was found dead at her home in London on Wednesday, August 25, 1926. Police reported that Scott, who was rumored to have had a brief romantic encounter with Valentino, may have taken her own life in grief at his death.

AROUND THE WORLD

The Roman newspaper *Osservatore Roman* reported that the spectacles surrounding Valentino's death "would make us laugh if they did not cause the most profound pity."

BEYOND THE GRAVE

Valentino wrote a book of poetry, *Day Dreams,* published in 1924 by the MacFadden Publishing Company.

A few months after Jean Acker filed for divorce, Valentino went to Mexico and married Natacha Rambova. When he returned to California he was charged with bigamy, since Acker had only received an "interlocutory decree"—the divorce would not be final for another year. Rambova and Valentino divorced and then had to wait until March 1923 to be officially remarried. The bigamy charges against the star were dropped.

SECRETS TO THE GRAVE

Valentino left no record of his intention to marry Pola Negri, although his doctor reported that the actor had spoken fondly of her on the day he died. Negri's performance as the idol's grief-stricken fiancée may have been the actress's best role.

Rumors claim that the riots surrounding Valentino's funeral had been orchestrated by Schenck and Valentino's manager in an attempt to increase interest in the star's final film and so add to the value of his estate.

THE HEREAFTER

Three months after Valentino's death, Natacha Rambova claimed that she had spoken with the star in the spirit world through the services of a medium. Rambova reported that Valentino had told her that he longed to be considered a "legitimate actor" and that he had met the great tenor Enrico Caruso in the astral plane; she said he never mentioned Pola Negri.

Friendly relations between Valentino's brother and the deceased actor's manager evaporated quickly when a court granted the manager sole executor privilege in October 1946. Alberto Guglielmi and his sister sued the estate, contesting the will.

In December 1926, the actor's two Hollywood homes and personal possessions were put up for auction. One of the homes, Falcon Lair, sold for $145,000, but his other property failed to sell. The actor's Arabian horse, which he had ridden in *The Son of the Sheik,* sold for $1,225.

On Christmas Eve, 1926, Pola Negri sued the estate of Rudolph Valentino for $15,000, which she claimed to have loaned her fiancé earlier in the year.

MAO ZEDONG

"Chairman Mao"

December 26, 1893–September 9, 1976

"A revolution is not a dinner party . . . A revolution is an act of violence."

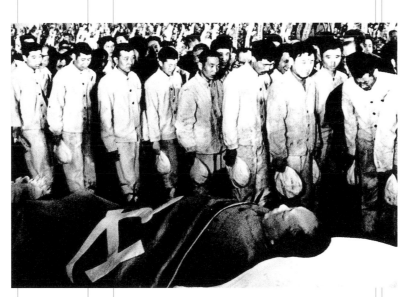

WORKERS FILE PAST CHAIRMAN **MAO**'S
BODY IN THE GREAT HALL OF THE PEOPLE.

VITAL STATISTICS

AGE AT DEATH: 82

CAUSE OF DEATH: Unconfirmed; possibly Parkinson's disease or Lou Gehrig's disease (amyotrophic lateral sclerosis)

SURVIVORS: His wife, Jiang Qing; two daughters, Li Min and Li Na; and a son, Mao An-ching

CLOSE CALLS: In 1927, Mao was captured by pro-nationalist troops but escaped before his execution.

HIS LIFE

China's most powerful political figure of the twentieth century, Mao Zedong was a complex character, full of contradictions and mystery. A man of revolutionary rhetoric and dogmatic discipline, the leader of China was also a voracious reader, a writer, and an expert on the ancient culture he publicly eschewed. The Communist leader was witty yet coarse, strong but ruthless.

Born to a peasant family in the Hunan province as the Manchu-Qing dynasty sputtered to an end, Mao Zedong grew up amid poverty and hardship; his stern father had improved the family's welfare through thrift and hard work. His compassionate Buddhist mother offset the father's harsh disposition. At the village school, Mao learned to read and write because his father wanted him to keep the family accounts. His early interest in reading would become a lifelong pursuit.

In 1911, as the Chinese nationalist movement was beginning, Mao defiantly cut off his pigtail and joined a local militia group. Two years later, after roaming the countryside with the militia, Mao furthered his education by reading the works of evolutionist Charles Darwin and French philosopher Jean Jacques Rousseau. In 1913, Mao attended school in Changsha, the Hunan provincial capital, where he studied for five years with an influential ethics professor and married the professor's daughter, Yang Kaihui. (Mao never considered his first wife, from an arranged childhood marriage, to be legitimate.) Upon graduation in 1918, Mao moved to Beijing and published his first article, which stressed the need for physical fitness training among all classes, a concept antithetical to most Chinese, who considered physical labor demeaning. It was a theme to which Mao would return countless times in his writings.

Introduced by his professor to one of the country's foremost intellectuals, Mao worked for him as a library assistant at Beijing University. There Mao awakened to the ideas of Marxism, bolshevism, and populism. By 1920, Mao Zedong had edited two journals and spent time organizing student radicals in Changsha, Shanghai, and Beijing. In Changsha, Mao organized the first communist group, and in Shanghai, with eleven other delegates, he formed the Chinese Communist Party (CCP) in July 1921.

The young revolutionary rose to power in the 1920s and 1930s as he sought to eradicate Western influences, which he felt degraded Chinese culture. Mao and the Communist Party joined the nationalist Kuomintang army of Sun Yat-sen, backed by the Soviet Union, opposing corrupt Chinese landlords and Western influences and striving to establish an independent China.

Upon Sun Yat-sen's death, General Chiang Kai-shek took over the army and, in a bloody massacre, ousted the Communist factions in 1927. Mao, who had returned to his home village before the slaughter, realized that his patriotic and populist beliefs were at odds with the Soviet agenda to support the nationalists. After the split with Chiang, Mao fled to the mountains and formed a Communist army to fight the Kuomintang militia. Between 1927 and 1934, Mao solidified control over the CCP and developed his vision for the country—that the peasantry, not the bourgeoisie, should have the power to command China. Through deprivation, physical fitness, and somewhat egalitarian command, Mao instilled discipline and strength and expanded his group of one thousand soldiers to more than one hundred thousand.

During this period, Mao's personal life also changed. In 1930, after the Kuomintang executed his second wife, Mao married the woman with whom he had lived for two years, He Zizhen, who was seventeen years his junior. She later accompanied her husband on what became known as "the Long March," one of the few women in the group, giving birth to one of their five children during their travels. In 1937 Mao divorced her; two years later he married his fourth wife, Jiang Qing.

In 1934's so-called Long March, the most daring act of his revolutionary career, Mao broke through nationalist army lines and marched six thousand miles into the mountains and caves of China in a guerrilla offensive lasting one year. Outnumbered and often without basic necessities, Mao's ragtag group of peasants overwhelmed the nationalists with superior tactics. He emerged as the clear leader of the Communist Party and earned a reputation for his steely command of his troops.

Japan's 1937 declaration of war on China forced the Communists into an alliance with the nationalist army to combat the intruders. But while Chiang fought the Japanese instead of the Communists, Mao regrouped his forces in the north and, claiming to fight the Japanese, instead published some of his most important articles on the principles of revolution. In 1942, Mao instituted the first "rectification" or thought-reform program for enlistees in the CCP. New members were indoctrinated with Mao's teachings, which stressed an emerging Chinese brand of Marxism.

Mao's army grew to more than a million men. At the end of World War II, as the Japanese threat receded, the two opposing factions resumed battle. Mao's forces pushed General Chiang out of the mainland to the island of Taiwan and on October 1, 1949, Mao Zedong established the People's Republic of China, with himself as the Communist Party chairman and chief of state.

Mao's vision provided the fundamentals for China's transformation from a country with a feudal economy to an industrialized nation—one of the most remarkable stories of the century. Adapting Marxist tenets, Mao followed the Soviet example of collectivization. When Stalin died in 1953, Mao became the dominant Marxist leader in the world. Chairman Mao turned his back on the Soviets, however, when Khrushchev denounced Stalin in 1956; Mao, in turn, denounced the Soviets as "revisionists."

By 1958, Mao had instituted "the Great Leap Forward," an attempt to incite moral zeal to produce agricultural products in newly formed communes; the program met with failure when disastrous weather conditions created a famine that killed 20 million people between 1959 and 1961. Thereafter, Mao's ascendancy declined, and his comrades removed him as chief of state although he retained control over the CCP.

With the assistance of a reeducated army under the command of Lin Biao, Mao enlisted young students to create the Red Guards, who routed out "revisionist" communists and terrorized citizens whom they accused of not living up to the communist ideals set forth in the Chairman's "little red book" of quotations. Mao's wife, Jiang Qing, was in charge of working the tenets of class struggle into traditional opera and movies. This Cultural Revolution, which lasted roughly from 1964 to 1969, returned to the grassroots fundamentals upon which Mao had built the Chinese revolution, reestablished his power and cult status, and created a sense of internal solidarity.

The People's Republic now turned its attention to modernization and industrialization. Mao knew that if he built up China's military strength and developed its economic prowess, the two superpowers—the Soviet Union and the United States—would be forced to take China seriously; with this goal in mind, he opened the door to relations with the United States in 1972.

Mao lived luxuriously, was attended by a large staff, and displayed a proclivity for sexual excess. He suffered from a debilitating, degenerative disease that kept him out of public view during the five years prior to his death, although he regularly met in private with foreign heads of state up until the end of his life. He died at 12:10 A.M. on Thursday, September 9, 1976. The Chinese government has never released information about Mao's disease or the cause of his death.

BEST KNOWN FOR: Establishment of the People's Republic of
                      China
FIRST JOB: Rice-field worker at age six
AVOCATION: Writing poetry and prose

RITES OF PASSAGE
THE PREPARATION

The People's Republic of China declared an official eight-day period of mourning beginning on Saturday, September 11. However, the government exerted tight control over those attending Mao's funeral. Thousands of security guards roped off one square mile of downtown Beijing that included Tiananmen Square and the Great Hall of the People, allowing only organized groups of mourners to be bussed in.

Newspapers, bordered in black, ran headlines such as LONG LIVE INVINCIBLE MARXISM-LENINISM AND MAO ZEDONG'S THOUGHTS. Loudspeakers on the streets carried funeral music and intermittently played the socialist anthem "Internationale."

Two days after Mao's death, workers removed a red neon sign from the top of the Bank of China building in the British colony of Hong Kong that proclaimed "Long Live Chairman Mao" in Chinese characters.

Two views of the decisions involved in the preparation of Chairman Mao's body have been published. In his book, *The Private Life of Chairman Mao,* personal physician Dr. Li Zhisui claims to have held Mao's hand as he died. Li's book states that he oversaw the process of embalming, which included injecting Mao's body with twenty-two liters of formaldehyde, almost a third more than required. Li reports that the work took ten hours to complete and that in the morning "Mao's face was as round as a ball, and his ears stuck out at right angles. Formaldehyde oozed from his pores."

Xu Jing, a curator at Mao's mausoleum in Tiananmen Square, who at the time of Mao's death was vice-director of the forensic medicine department of the Chinese Institute of Medical Sciences, reports in her book, *The Resting Place of the Great,* that thousands of people contributed to creating the chairman's eternal resting place and the seeming lifelike repose. She wrote that it was Prime Minister Hua Guofeng who decided on the position of Mao's arms and that the entire Central Committee was involved in selecting Mao's light gray suit. Xu's account reports that Mao's widow, upset with the results of the embalming, abducted the body shortly after the September 12 service to an underground bomb shelter, where the chairman's remains were subjected to herbal baths, chemicals, and refrigeration.

PAYING RESPECTS

On Saturday and Sunday, September 11 and 12, more than one hundred thousand Chinese visited Mao Zedong's bier in the Great Hall of the People; by September 17 nearly half a million people had paid tribute to the founder of modern China. The orderly crowds waited in lines four abreast to pass the chairman's bier. Chairman Mao lay with his hands by his side on a catafalque draped in white fabric and surrounded by cypress branches, a Chinese symbol of eternity. A glass box enclosed his corpse, which was bathed in yellow light.

On Monday, September 13, the Chinese permitted foreigners to pay respects for the first time since Mao's death. The first admitted were Albanian students studying at Beijing University. Former defense secretary James Schlesinger and his wife, who were visiting China at the invitation of the Chinese People's Institute of Foreign Affairs, represented the United States. Ironically, Mao had expressed interest in meeting Mr. Schlesinger just two days before his death.

THE FUNERAL

THE SERVICE On Saturday, September 11, a memorial service that included fifteen of the sixteen living Politburo members, a significant sign of China's continued unity, gathered in Beijing to commence the eight-day period of mourning. The service was televised in China and beamed via satellite to Hong Kong. Mao's widow, Jiang Qing, wore a black headdress and was included among the official state mourners.

An estimated million people attended a formal memorial rally for Chairman Mao held on Saturday, September 18, marking the end of the official period of mourning. The rally began with a call for China's 800 million citizens to stand and observe three minutes of silence for Mao Zedong. The Chinese

Communist Party and government officials excluded foreigners from the services, reestablishing a centuries-old tradition of isolation. The televised event assured the people of continuity in the leadership of the Chinese Communist Party, as Prime Minister Hua Guofeng delivered a eulogy from Beijing's Gate of Heavenly Peace in Tiananmen Square.

FINAL RESTING PLACE Chinese rulers are traditionally cremated. At the time of his death, Mao's wishes for the disposal of his remains were not known. Chinese Communist Party officials at one point reported that Chairman Mao had preferred cremation but that "the people" did not favor it.

Hence, in the great tradition of Soviet Communist leaders Lenin and Stalin, Mao Zedong was embalmed and placed on display in a glass-enclosed mausoleum, which was opened in 1981. Chairman Mao's remains are secured in an earthquake- and terrorist-proof building equipped with an elevator that lowers the body into a climate-controlled subterranean room each evening, allowing technicians to monitor any deterioration, coloration, or shrinkage of the cadaver.

NEWS OF THE DAY
SEPTEMBER 10, 1976
**MAO TSE-TUNG DIES IN BEIJING AT 82;
LEADER OF RED CHINA REVOLUTION;
CHOICE OF SUCCESSOR IS UNCERTAIN**

**RADAR IMAGES FROM VENUS DEPICT
VAST AREA OF POSSIBLE LAVA FLOW**

AROUND THE WORLD
In Taiwan, a stronghold of nationalist Chinese sentiment, the news of Mao's death was greeted by cheers.

China rejected messages of condolence from the Soviet Union and East European communist parties, explaining that China did not recognize the communist parties in Eastern Europe and rejected the Soviet Union's communist party.

In New York City on Sunday, September 19, twenty-five hundred people filled Hunter College Auditorium to attend a tribute to Chairman Mao Zedong, sponsored by the China People's Friendship Association. Professor Wang Hao of Rockefeller University delivered the key memorial address under a large portrait of Mao that was flanked by white and yellow floral tributes.

BEYOND THE GRAVE

One month after her husband's death, Jiang Qing and her "Gang of Four" associates were arrested by the Communist Party for crimes committed during the Cultural Revolution. She was jailed in 1976 and condemned to death in 1981. In 1983 her sentence was commuted to life imprisonment. She died, reportedly by her own hand, in 1991.

The cult of Mao still thrives in the flea markets of China, where shopkeepers are no longer arrested for selling likenesses of China's former leader. As the twentieth century came to a close, an entire industry arose selling his image on clothing, calendars, tie clips, buttons, hats, and clocks.

ODD COINCIDENCES

On September 12, 1976, Macy's department store ran a full-page advertisement for its "White Flower Days" sale featuring an illustration of a giant panda smelling a white flower. Giant pandas live only in China, where white flowers are considered a traditional sign of mourning.

SECRETS TO THE GRAVE

According to Dr. Li, fear that the embalming efforts might fail led the team of technicians to create a wax replica of Mao Zedong. Dr. Li claims never to have learned whether the real or wax Mao was placed on display in the glass mausoleum.

THE HEREAFTER

Moderates under the leadership of Deng Xiaoping supplanted Mao's handpicked successor, Hua Guofeng. Deng, a party insider who had worked beside Mao in the Long March, had twice been banished by Mao, most recently in 1976, shortly before the chairman's death.

Deng Xiaoping led the People's Republic of China into a period of post-Mao economic expansionism, opening trade with the West. In 1981, Deng orchestrated a reevaluation of Mao Zedong, criticizing the Cultural Revolution. In 1982 the constitution was revised to ban personality cults and stress economic achievement over class struggle. By the mid-1980s, the government had removed many statues of Mao in public squares.